My Life Story

My Life Story

The first 30 years

OLIMPIO GUIDI

Archway Publishing books may be ordered through booksellers or by contacting:

Archway Publishing
1663 Liberty Drive
Bloomington, IN 47403
www.archwaypublishing.com
844-669-3957

ISBN: 978-1-6657-4238-2 (sc)
ISBN: 978-1-6657-4239-9 (e)

Library of Congress Control Number: 2023907054

Print information available on the last page.

Archway Publishing rev. date: 4/17/2023

Contents

Preface

I would like to dedicate this simple but sincere book to a dear friend, a retired US Navy Commander, Hugh "Toby" Haynsworth who worked with me on this book project and provided me with valuable assistance in gathering information and in 1995 he also visited and toured Sicily with me for a week to gather additional information. Sadly, four years ago my very dear friend Toby, a great human being, a good friend and mentor died before we could put this book together but I did have his valuable written input and recall our many conversations about Sicily that I was able to use. I met Toby in 1970 when he took over as the Supply Officer at the US Naval Air Faculty (NAF) Sigonella, Sicily where I worked. I had recently been discharged from 10 years of active duty in the US Navy and, following my discharge, I accepted a temporary civilian entry position in the Sigonella base Supply Department. Since my family and I loved living in Italy/Sicily and the cost of living was very reasonable, I decided to accept a low-ranking GS-3 position. In addition to loving the area, we also had many great Sicilian friends and memories there. As I discuss in this book, soon after his arrival as the Supply Officer, Toby had a serious talk with me concerning my future civil service employment. I could see that he was sincerely concerned for my temporary employment status and I really appreciated his interest and concern. Soon after our discussion he arranged for me to go to Ft Lee, VA for a transportation management course and then to Washington, DC to take a civil service exam, which I did. On my return to Sicily I obtained civil service career status and received a promotion to GS-9, transportation officer. Toby was not only instrumental in getting me permanent civilian status, he also encouraged me to take evening college courses. I was not certain I could succeed in college since I had not even graduated from high school, although I had taken a test and received a high school equivalency diploma. He gave me the confidence in my abilities and with his encouragement (push) I enrolled in the University of Maryland overseas Sigonella campus and in four years, while at Sigonella I earned an Associate (AA) degree and continued taking other courses. I continued taking college courses after my return to the US and attended night classes at the University of Maryland Pentagon campus. I completed the required courses and in 1979 and received a BS degree in business administration at age 38. Thanks to Toby believing in me and his encouragement, I went on to have a very successful civil service career, retiring as a GS-13. Not bad for an immigrant, who did not speak English until age 15 and a high school dropout.

Toby loved the game of soccer that he had developed while stationed at the US Embassy in Madrid, Spain and became a fan of the great Real Madrid soccer team. When he came to Sicily he joined me at games at the Catania stadium and he became a big fan of the Catania soccer team. With his homemade banner "Forza Catania, Sigonella e con te" (Go Catania Sigonella is with you) we attended most home games at the Catania Cibali stadium. Many other Americans from the base, including his deputy and another good friend, LCDR Ed Hernandez and his son Mike joined us and attended most home games as well as some away games. Toby soon became a favorite with the local fans and the Catania paper, La Sicilia wrote a great article about the "American who was an avid Catania fan". It was a fun two years with Toby while he was in Sicily. About 25 year later Toby, his wife and I went to Catania with his original banner and attended a Catania home game with the banner in front of us, like the old days. We received a standing ovation and another great article in the local paper, La Sicilia.

I cannot say enough about Toby. He was, most of all, a dear sincere friend who was more than instrumental in what I consider was my very successful civil service career. Four years ago Toby died and it really saddened me. I lost my very best friend, I really miss having our daily email contacts. We always had interesting discussions and, although we did not always agree, we would always end our email conversations with Toby writing "let's just agree to disagree." I will forever be grateful to Toby for his professional support but most of all for his sincere friendship, he was the best friend I ever had – thank you Toby for being a dear friend and for all you did for me, it was a lot of fun spending time with you. I really miss talking to you via email and think of you often. I will never forget you. Although I tried not to be too repetitive, some discussions that I have included in this book were also part of my first book, "My Life Story".

Chapter 1

I was born Jun 14 1941 in the Republic of San Marino, a mountainous landlocked microstate, completely surrounded by central Italy. San Marino is located between the Italian provinces of Emilia-Romagna and Marche and close to the Adriatic Sea coast. San Marino rightfully claims to be the world's oldest and smallest republic (republic, not just a country but a republic). The Most Serene Republic of San Marino is one city-state that was not a great power or important, it simply just wanted to be left alone, and that is why they chose to become and remain a country in the first place. According to tradition San Marino was founded in the year 301 AD by Marinus, a Christian stonemason from Croatia who was seeking refuge from religious persecution in Croatia and fled to Rimini, Italy where he worked as a stone cutter and remained there until he decided to take refuge on Mt Titano, a few kilometers from Rimini. The current population of San Marino is 33,400, the national language is Italian and the main religion is Roman Catholic. The life expectancy is 78 years for males (which I already exceeded) and 85 years for females. San Marino is a developed country and one of the safest and most interesting countries one could ever visit where the crime rate is very low, almost nonexistent. The capital of the country, is also called San Marino, and is known for its medieval walled old town and the narrow cobblestone streets and it retains much of its historic architecture. The three towers, castle like citadels dating to the 11th

century, sit on top of three peaks on Mount Titano and dominates the San Marino's landscape.

I took this picture of Mt Titano

San Marino has been occupied by foreign militaries only three times in its long history, each time for only short periods. Two of these periods were in the feudal era. In 1503, Cesare Borgia occupied the Republic until the death of his father some months later. On 4 June 1543, Fabiano di Monte San Savino, nephew of the later Pope Julius III, attempted to conquer the republic in a plan involving 500 infantry men and some cavalry. The group failed as they got lost in a dense fog, which the Sammarinese attributed to Saint Quirinus since it happened on his feast day that is now celebrated annually. San Marino faced many potential threats during the feudal period, so a treaty of protection was signed in 1602 with Pope Clement VIII, which came into force in 1631. On 17 October 1739, Cardinal Giulio Alberoni, Papal Governor of Ravenna, used military force to occupy the country, imposed a new constitution, and attempted to force the Sammarinesi to submit to the government of the Papal States. It is believed, however, that he was probably acting contrary to the orders of Pope Clement XII. Civil disobedience occurred and clandestine notes, appealing for justice, were written and sent to the Pope. On 5 February 1740, three and one half months after the occupation began, the Pope recognized San Marino's rights to its independence. As a result, 5 February, the feast day of Saint

Agata, is celebrated in recognition for being freed on that day and Saint Agata is also one of the patron saints of San Marino. Note: Saint Agata is from Catania and of course is also the patron saint of that city. I lived with my family in her home town of Catania for 12 wonderful years.

an image of Sant Agata I took in a San Marino church

After Napoleon's Italian campaign, San Marino found itself on the border between the Kingdom of Italy and its long-time ally, the Papal States. Napoleon agreeing with the ideals of liberty and humanity extolled in San Marino's humble founding, wrote in recognition of its cultural value offering to extend its territory according to its needs. While grateful for his offer of territorial expansion, San Marino politely declined, they just wanted to remain who they were, a small independent republic and be left alone. Napoleon also issued orders that exempted all San Marino citizens from any type of taxation. The mystery behind Napoleon's friendly treatment of San Marino may be better understood in light of the French Revolution (1789–1799) where France was undergoing drastic political reform. At this time, the Republic of San Marino and the recently established First French Republic (est. 1792) were ideologically aligned. The San Marino state was recognized by Napoleon in the Treaty of Tolentino in 1797 and by the Congress of Vienna in 1815. Napoleon is viewed favorably by the Sammarinesi and one of the main streets in the capital is named Via Napoleone Bonaparte.

In 1825 and 1853, attempts were made by the Papal States to submit San Marino to its authority but it failed. San Marino also did not want to join other states in a unified Italy and just wanted to be left out of the Italian unification plan and desired to remain a free and independent country and just be left alone. This wish was honored by Giuseppe Garibaldi in gratitude for the protection and hospitality San Marino provided him, his wife Anita and his troops keeping them from being arrested. Garibaldi confirmed and supported San Marino's independence. When Garibaldi was granted the honorary citizenship of San Marino he declared "I am proud to be a citizen of this virtuous republic" and on 13 June 1864 stated "I thank you for this great gift that reminds me of your generous hospitality. The Sammarinesi admired Italy's desire for freedom and for this reason protected Garibaldi and his troops. I have included a picture I took of the statue of Garibaldi in the capital city of San Marino.

In the spring of 1861, shortly before the beginning of the American Civil War, the government of San Marino wrote a letter to United States President, Abraham Lincoln, proposing an "alliance" between the two democratic nations and offering Lincoln honorary San Marino citizenship which he accepted, writing in reply that "Although your dominion is small, your State is nevertheless one of the most honored, in all of history." This is a picture I took of a bust of Lincoln which is located in the Government palace. A stamp was also issued in his honor and one of the main streets of San Marino is named Via Abramo Lincoln.

A picture I took of a statue of Lincoln located in the San Marino government building

Chapter 2

I n World War 1, on 23 May 1915, while Italy declared war on Austria-Hungary, San Marino decided to remain neutral. Italy, fearful that San Marino could harbor Austrian spies who could be given access to its territory, tried and failed to convince San Marino to establish a detachment of Carabinieri on San Marino territory. Following San Marino's refusal to allow Italian Carabinieri on its territory, Italy suspended all their vital support to San Marino for telephone and telegraph communications. San Marino was also not directly involved in the Second World War although in September 1940, press reports claimed that San Marino may have declared war on Britain in support of Italy, a claim that was denied by the San Marino government. San Marino did provide refuge for over 100,000 Italian civilians who sought safety from the war raging in Italy, all around San Marino. This was an enormous relief effort by the 15,000 inhabitants of a very small and, at that time, poor country, but they (we) did it.

Italian refugees camping out in San Marino. This picture was
given to me and would like it published, if possible

One of the victims of the bombing was the San Marino railway. The "Ferrovia Rimini–San Marino" was an electrified narrow gauge railway that after four years of construction became operational on 12 June 1932. It connected the Italian city of Rimini to the capital of the Republic of San Marino. The railway was closed, as discussed below, following the British bombing of San Marino on 26 June 1944. Since most of the tracks have been either removed or paved over the railroad was never re-activated. The railroad was 32 km long and there were 12 tunnels and 6 major bridges within the borders of San Marino. During the war one blue electric car was kept in a tunnel where it remained for 67 years after the war. The electric car was subsequently restored to its original state by a citizen's initiative. The San Marino terminal station with the original blue electric car is now a tourist attraction.

a picture I took of a blue electric car on display for tourists

Many older San Marino citizens, like my grandfather Cristofero, were hoping and predicting the railway would be restored but to date it has not happened. However, I recently read a report where there is an initiative to bring back the train service although I believe, even if it's true, it will take some time to lay the tracks, and restore the tunnels and bridges. If it happened it would be wonderful and my grandfather would be very happy.

On 26 June 1944 when I was 3 years old, San Marino was bombed by the British Royal Air Force which mistakenly believed the country had been overrun by German forces and was being used to amass and store ammunitions. As a result of the bombing, as noted above, the San Marino railway system was permanently destroyed and at least 63 civilians were killed. On the same day the Sammarinese government emphasized that at that time, no German military installations or equipment were located on its sovereign territory. The British government later admitted the bombing was not justified and that it had been executed on receipt of erroneous information and after the war they paid for some (not nearly enough) reparations. San Marino's hope to escape further involvement was shattered on 27 July 1944 when Germany announced that San Marino sovereignty could not be respected if it became necessity for German troops and vehicles to transit its territory. Fears were confirmed on 30 July when a German medical corps colonel presented himself with an order for the requisition of two public buildings to establish a German military hospital. The German army for a time occupied the neutral Republic of San Marino. They were then attacked by Allied forces on 17–20 September 1944 during Allied Italian Campaign. During this period, my family and I spent many days in a train tunnel when San Marino was being bombed and, although I was only a little more than 3 years old, I remember and recall some of the bombings and our great parents lying on my sister and me to protect us from the falling debris.

The Germans and Allies clashed on San Marino's soil in late September 1944 at the Battle of Monte Pulito. The Germans were defeated and Allied troops occupied San Marino but only for about two months before restoring the Republic's sovereignty. As young as I was, I will always remember how kind many American soldiers were, giving us kids some of their Spam rations which was one of the main rations for soldiers and also distributed some candy. After the war we received some food aid, like sacks of wheat and flower from the United States government which was very much appreciated by the hungry citizens of San Marino. For many years after the war Spam remained one of my favorite foods until I became a vegetarian. Most of my relatives were farmers and had access to more food than my family since we were not famers. I often visited my relative's extended family that was living and working on a large farm. My grandmother, my mom's mother a widow, lived with them and almost every day she would hide a couple of eggs in the hay stack for me to find and take home. I really appreciated my nonna's kindness. I have included a picture of my grandfather, uncles and my many cousins working on the large farm; hardworking, honest farmers. And also a picture of my wonderful "piccola nonna".

I also had many cousins living on the farm that I was close to. I was particularly close to one cousin in particular, Giannina, shown in the middle of a picture I have attached. She was a tomboy and could climb trees with ease, much better than me. When there was fruit on the trees, Gianna would climb almost to the top and pick fruit which she shared with me. We had a lot of fun as kids and remained friends for life. Gianna and her husband Gigi immigrated to Detroit and moved next door to my family. A few years later they returned to San Marino. Unfortunately Giannina passed away several years ago and I still miss her. I also had a great relationship with all my adult relatives especially my dad's sister, my Zia (aunt) Norina and his brother Zio (uncle) Leo. Norina was a great nurse at the one and only San Marino hospital and she was of great help to me when I had an appendectomy. Norina was a single mother, very unusual at that time, and my great dad, her brother, and my generous mother were very supportive and helped with caring for her daughter Ginetta who was the same age as my sister Rita. I have enclosed a picture taken soon after the end of the war of me with my sister Rita and my cousin Ginetta.

My zia worked at the hospital in the capital city of San Marino where she lived. She lived in a building that had an indoor community bathroom that I found fantastic since it was the first time I remember using an indoor bathroom. She also had a radio, something I had never seen let alone heard before and I was amazed. The first time I heard someone speaking on the radio I went outside to see who was talking and was surprised there was no one there. A year later, when we moved to an apartment with electricity, and since my dad had saved enough money to purchase a radio we could now listen to our own radio. For the first time in my life I became aware of the outside world around me, it was for me very exciting. I remember hearing when Elisabeth became the Queen of England in February 1952 and learning about the British Royal Family. The radio for me was a life changing experience that I appreciated very much.

Between and after the two wars the San Marino economy really suffered and many citizens were forced to immigrate to other European countries and the Americas to make a living. Today there are more than 15,000 San Marino citizens spread throughout the world, with large concentrations in Italy, France, the United States (many in Detroit, like my family), and South America, especially Argentina where my grandfather, immigrated for a couple of years around 1920. In spite of the war and other hardships, including some hunger that I experienced as a child, I had, what I still consider a good and happy childhood and was fortunate to have great parents, siblings and neighbors and a lot of good friends my age. My father was a kind, a humble, hardworking good man and a skilled carpenter. Although he did not earn much he always had a job and worked hard to support the family. My mother was also a hard worker who took good care of the family as I discuss below. Initially we lived in a two room home with a dirt floor, no electricity or running water and, of course, no central heat in the winter and no indoor bathroom. We were even too poor to have an outhouse, so we went in the fields. One of my jobs was to go to a well about half a kilometer from our home and fetch water several times a day. The water was for cooking and bathing.

Although not easy I was proud and happy to be of some help to my family. I was very happy in the winter when we had heavy snow falls we would gather the snow in front of our house and melt it for water so on those days I did not have to go to the well. In spite of obvious hardships I still considered myself very fortunate to have had a great extended family, loving parents who took good care of us – we were their number one priority. I also had a great sister and then a brother came along. We also had outstanding neighbors and many great friends who helped and we took care and looked out for each other as needed. A great example was shortly after I was born my mother experienced some health issues and after 2 months could not continue to breast feed me. At that time there was no baby formula or any kind of baby food available, (even if it were available, my family could not have afforded to buy it) therefore babies were breast fed until they could eat solid food. Given my mom's condition the neighborhood ladies, who were also breastfeeding their own infants, stepped forward and took turns to breast feed me until I could eat solid food. I know that I probably owe those kind and great ladies my life. The first time I returned to San Marino, 10 years after immigrating to the US, I visited the ladies who had breast fed me to thank them personally for what they had done for me. In our poor but great small neighborhood it was common practice to help each other as those ladies did it for me and I will be forever grateful to them. My dear mother, along with the other neighborhood ladies worked full time just taking care of the home without any of the current labor saving convinces like a vacuum cleaner, washing machines or even running water in the home, let alone hot water. The ladies would do the laundry in a nearby creek washing the clothes in cold water by hand on a big rock which was, of course, very labor intensive and took a lot of time. I have included a picture of my great, hardworking, and dedicated mom – Eva.

Of course in the winter it was usually impossible to use the creek so my mom washed our clothes in the house using a large container (the one also used for our baths) and a board. The one and only appliance in our house was a wood burning stove that was used for all the cooking and to heat some water to do the dishes and in the winter provide limited heat for the two room house. My father would bring home wood from his carpenter shop and other places. I helped by gathering additional wood from the countryside. It was a team effort in order to have sufficient wood for the stove that was so important to my family. We were very grateful to have this stove. My mom also heated water on the stove for our weekly baths. All this was, of course, also very labor intensive. To warm our bed my mom gathered hot coals from the stove and put it in a container and placed the container under the sheets before we went to bed. I remember how initially, after using the bed warmer, the bed was nice and warm but during the night it got cold and in the morning I rushed out of bed quickly got dressed, I did not waste much time. I have included pictures of a wood burning stove like the one we had and the bed prepared for a bed warmer, as noted above, with coals from the wood burning stove.

We lived almost 2 kilometers from the center of the small town of Domagnano where the school and church were located and where my dad had his carpenter shop. Of course my father had to walk to his shop year around. I remember when he bought an old bicycle to go to work and my mom was not very happy since we had a limited amount of money. Of course I also had to walk to the school year around in all kinds of weather. I like to tell my kids that I walked up the hill both ways even with snow to go to school. As I recall, we did not have any snow days. I have included a picture of my third grade class with our great teacher, Gennaro who I remember fondly, taken in Domagnano, San Marino in 1951.

Chapter 3

Although, as noted above, my family was very poor I had nonetheless what I considered a very happy childhood, with loving and caring parents, a great sister and then brother as well as many good neighbors and friends who always helped and looked out for each other. Of course I had all the childhood diseases since at the time, at least for my family in San Marino, there were no vaccines available. I contacted but was able to overcome all the childhood illnesses and survived with, what I believe, was probably a stronger immune system which came in handy in later life. I experienced a serious medical problem at age 10 and it was determined I needed an appendectomy. I remember the operation vividly since they used very limited local anesthesia for the surgery. I was not put to sleep, and was awake for the entire and painful procedure. While they were at it, the doctors, at my mother's request, removed a birth mark above my left eye. In spite of all this, I considered myself lucky and am grateful for the medical care I received.

The age difference with my younger sister Rita is only 14 months so we grew up together and looked out for each other and, generally speaking, got along well. I have attached a picture of our confirmation which we celebrated together.

We were both very happy when in 1948 our brother Marino was born and joined the family. As noted above, and I want to stress, my great parents took very good care of me and my sister and Marino when he joined the family and we all chipped in caring for him. Of course we did not have any store bought toys and managed to stay busy by doing cut outs and playing outside. As discussed above, I had a great aunt, my zia Norina who was a very skillful nurse and lived in the city in a small modest apartment. Norina would visit us often and when she could afford it brought us some torrone (hard almond candy), something I loved but only had it when Norina brought it. I loved visiting Norina in her small apartment in the city since it was located in a building which had, as noted above, a community indoor bathroom.

In our small neighborhood I had many friends and we enjoyed playing together when I did not have chores, like hauling water from a well several times a day. As hard as life was, I did have some fond memories as a child to include having a dog by the name of

Reno. A big mixed breed black dog who followed me wherever I went. Since we had a very limited amount of food Reno ate whatever he was offered. In addition to my dog I also befriended the pigs my dad purchased in February of every year. The pigs would follow me when I was outside and were as smart as my dog and I really considered them my pets. The sad part for me was that a pig would be butchered yearly in order for my family to have food. When the day of butchering came I went as far away from home as I could so as not to hear the poor animal squeal – it was for me very sad. Every family in our neighborhood had a pig and the men took turns assisting each other in processing the meat since at that time in San Marino there were no refrigerators so all the meat not cooked following the butchering and had to be processed in order to keep it from deteriorating. Processed meat is considered to be any meat which has been modified in order to either improve its taste but mostly to extend its shelf life without refrigeration which, as noted above, at that time we did not have. In fact until I was 9 and we moved to town we did not even have electricity. Methods of meat processing include salting, curing fermentation smoking, and/or the addition of chemical preservatives (something not available at the time). Processed meat, cured by my dad and neighbors, was limited to pork. Methods of meat processing includes all the processes that change fresh meat into cured meat. Meat processing began many years ago as soon as people realized that salting preserves and prolongs the life of fresh meat. It is not known when this first took place; however, the process of salting and sun-drying was recorded in Ancient Egypt, while using ice and snow is credited to early Romans.

As discussed above, when I was 9 my family moved to an apartment in back of the church in the center of the town of Domagnano. Although the apartment was sparse with only the basics it was a big improvement over the house we left. For starters it had a cement floor and not a dirt floor and also had limited electricity for lights and more importantly it gave me the opportunity to listen to a radio as much as I wanted and, as noted above, I became familiar with the outside world, thanks to our radio. In early 1952 I remember hearing that the king of England had died and now that country had a queen – Elizabeth II. We did not have running water in the house and no central heat. We did have a small outhouse although I often preferred using the field. The only appliance we had, like in the other house, was a wood/coal burning stove that was used for cooking, heating water and provided limited heat in the cold San Marino winters. Although we did not have running water in the apartment, there was a fountain very close to our house so it was much easier for me to bring home water, a big improvement from having to walk a kilometer to go to/from the well. My mother also used the fountain to wash my face and hands before going to school. Many times in the winter she had to break the ice to get the water to wash me. I do remember it was cold.

Like in the other house, once a week my mother would heat some water on the same wood burning stove we had in the other house and bathed us in a large metal tub that was also used, as noted above, to do laundry in the winter. One other great advantage of moving was that we lived only a block from my school, no more long walks up the hill in all kinds of weather. My father who, as noted above, was a skilled carpenter had his carpenter shop in the square in front of where we lived so things got easier for him as well. It was for sure a great improvement in our simple lives and was very much appreciated. I have included a picture of my great, hardworking, humble father Antonio.

I was fortunate to have so many good friends and when I wasn't busy doing chores, I spent time with my friends. One of my best friends was named Marino, like many men are named in San Marino in honor of the founding father and patron sanit. Marino's dad had a grocery store so he had more access to food than I did and he was very generous and often brought me some slices of tasty "mortadella" for me to eat which I really appreciated. Since my dad's carpenter shop was in the square in front of our house I spent time with him, helping where I could. In spite of some obvious hardships I was happy with what we had and mostly for my many good friends and great family. I enjoyed going to school and learning so many new things. As discussed above, I kept up with the news via our radio that I really loved. I repeat that, although we were poor. I had what I considered a very happy childhood.

Another thing I really enjoyed very much when I was young was the yearly "Giro d'Italia" bicycle race that is still a yearly event in Italy. The best cyclists in the world take part in this almost one month race, usually in May. The giro takes riders around Italy from north to south including the islands. The race also came through San Marino where fans could line the roads to cheer their favorite participant. My uncle Leo who would take me to see the race and cheer for our favorite racer. Mine was Fausto Coppi his was Gino Bartali, both champion racers. It was a lot of fun teasing each other and I looked forward to the race and appreciated very much my uncle taking me to see it. Attached is a picture of the greats Fausto Coppi and Gino Bartali.

I just read that in 2023 the Giro di Francia (France tour) will go through San Marino, which is a first. I would love to be there to see it

Although San Marino is not a member of the European Union, it has an agreement with Italy to use the euro as its currency and, by arrangement with the Council of the European Union, is also granted the right to mint and use its own designs on the national side on a limited number of euro coins. Tourism and light industry dominates the economy of this 61 square kilometer (23.6 square miles) republic, which plays host to more than three million visitors every year. In 1992 San Marino joined the United Nations. In 2009 the San Marino government said it would take action to ensure the country complied with OECD rules on financial transparency in order to be removed from tax haven "grey list".

After moving in the house in back of the church, as discussed above, our life became much simpler and I enjoyed myself even more since I had a many friends and, of course, our many relatives who ran a farm where I often visited them and, as noted above, my piccola nonna always had some eggs for me to take home.

Chapter 4

In 1951 my father applied to emigrate to the United Sates and was soon authorized to move there. Soon after he received the authorization he departed for Detroit where he joined my uncle Leo, who had emigrated years earlier, and other relatives who lived there. The move was very difficult for him as well as the rest of the family who remained in San Marino. I really missed my great dad since we had never been apart before. It was tough especially for my mom and my siblings as well. A year later, the rest of the family was granted permission to emigrate to the United States and I reluctantly (did not have a choice) left my native Republic of San Marino with my mom, sister and brother to immigrate to the United States of America and join my father who had, as noted above, immigrated there a year earlier and had established a residence in Detroit, MI. I had my 11th birthday on 14 June 1952 on board the passenger ship, the SS Saturnia. It was for me a very interesting 12 day trip from Genova, Italy to New York and I had many new experiences on the ship. For starters I had a selection of more food than I had ever seen in my entire life when we often did not have sufficient food and for sure never more than one choice. Some of the food served on the ship was new to me like, for example, bananas that I had never even seen a banana in my life, let alone taste one. We were on the ship for the feast of the Corpus Domini, which literally translates to the body and blood of Christ, an important Catholic holiday. Since most passengers were Roman

Catholic there was a solemn mass and procession on the main deck. Since (believe it or not) I was an altar boy, I assisted with the mass and that's me in one of the pictures with the incent holder and my sister Rita walking in front of the precession.

We arrived in New York and were assisted in clearing US customs and taken to New York Grand Central Station to board a train that evening for Detroit where my father was waiting for us. We were left there alone and spent most of the day at the train station, hungry not able to understand or speak one word of English. My father had sent us some dollars but I had no idea what food I could buy. Fortunately for me a very nice and kind African-American gentleman who was selling food could see how confused and scared I was and, although we could not talk to each other, he understood what I needed and was kind enough to prepare four sandwiches and some soda. I will never forget the kindness of that very understanding gentleman. I can say that my first experience with an American was more than positive and I will never forget his kindness, God bless him. I appreciated having the sandwiches since we were very hungry. For the first time in my life I tasted mayonnaise and I really did not like it but was very happy to have something to eat and drink. The move was very traumatic for me. First of all, I was very upset to leave my friends and the many relatives in San Marino. Although there we were very poor, as noted above, I had a decent and generally speaking a happy childhood with many of friends and relatives. Also it was not easy coming to a country where I did not know the language or customs. The only good thing was being reunited with my dear and great father that I had missed a lot. A family picture, soon after our arrival in Detroit taken in front of the house my father had purchased in the Oakwood neighborhood of Detroit.

Chapter 5

I spent the summer working with my dad on a construction sites doing light manual labor. I enjoyed that work and being with my dad so I was disappointed when I was told that I would have to quit my job and enroll in school at the end of summer. I still could not speak or understand any English and going to our local Hunter Elementary school, not knowing the language was, to say the least, very stressful and difficult. Also, my mom dressed me like she did in San Marino, with Italian style clothes, as shown in one of the pictures.

The other children made fun of me and some of the boys bullied me, it was not easy and I was, to say the least, miserable and confused and really missed my friends and life in San Marino even more. Thankfully, after two weeks of struggling at our local school my sister and I were sent to a specialized outstanding school for foreign students in downtown Detroit where we felt more inclusive since all students were foreign and were in the same boat as we were and none bullied me. It was really a good school with some outstanding specialized teachers and we learned to speak and understand enough English to enable us to return, in a couple of months, to our local Hunter school. Unfortunately, at our local school I was placed in the second grade at the age 11, not a good situation for me. At first I had struggled with the language but I worked hard and little by little and attending summer school, in a couple of years I made enough progress to be placed in a grade more consistent with my age.

On my return to my local school I was once again bullied, especially by a boy name Ron. He would push me against the lockers and demand my lunch money while his friends watched and laughed. I usually gave up my lunch money to avoid being beat up. That was until one day when, I really don't know what came over me, but at a certain point I jumped on Ron and began punching him. It took some of his friends some time to pull me off. After that incident I was not bothered again by Ron or any of his friends.

School was a struggle having to learn a new language but I made it and graduated from elementary school at age 14. I then applied for and was accepted to attend Cass Technical high school in downtown Detroit, a great trade school where I elected to study architectural drafting in the hope that I could someday design homes for my father who was a skilled carpenter, to build. It was an interesting and rewarding experience and I enjoyed the classes; however, after two semesters when I struggled to maintain an acceptable grade average, I was transferred to our local high school, Southwestern High School. In addition to going to school almost year around, I always had more than one part time job like a 5 am paper route, bagging groceries in an Italian grocery store, Lora Provision, after school and on weekends set pins until 2 am at the Oakwood Bowling Lanes near my home. While working at the bowling alley I was often hit by flying pins and still have scars in my lower legs from getting hit. At age16 I got a great new job at Cunningham Drug store in downtown Detroit delivering prescription drugs to patients in the downtown area. I also had a Saturday job at Shoe fair showing potential customders shoes. This is a picture of me at my Cunningham and Shoe fair jobs with my suit a lot of hair.

At Cunningham Drug store, in addition to delivering prescription drugs to customers who worked in various offices in the downtown area, I also was responsible to prepare packages to mail. It was a very interesting job and I enjoyed it very much. At Shoe fair I assisted customers in selecting and trying out shoes. It was also an interesting experience which helped me dealing with people, I did acquire some important "people skills" at both jobs.

Chapter 6

When I turned 18 I completed the 12th grade but was short three classes from being able to graduate and would have to return for the fall semester to earn a High School diploma. At this point I was burned out and tired of going to school year around and working 2-3 part time jobs. Instead of enrolling for another semester, I decided to join the US Navy, which I did in September 1959. Prior to reporting for my first duty station – boot camp - I took the test and became a very proud US citizen.

Once I was sworn in the US Navy I attended the two month US Navy Boot Camp at Great Lakes, Illinois. Most of my shipmates complained of how hard and difficult boot camp was for them. For me, after working three or four odd jobs since age 13, and going to school full-time year around, it was a life changing improvement and a piece of cake which I very much enjoyed. I especially enjoyed the friendships I made, the marching, the firefighting drills as well the many other military activities. It was a very interesting for me and great learning experience which I appreciated and it really helped my self-esteem. Towards the end of boot camp I was asked my preference of what I wanted to do in the Navy. I asked to be given any assignment that did not involve handling firearms. I was happy to be offered and I gladly accepted to attend Hospital Corps School to become a US Navy Hospital Corpsman or Medic. In boot camp I was designated as student Company Commander of our graduation formation. I appreciated this honor and did my very best shouting out orders. The Boot Camp graduation ceremony was great and was attended by my parents and girlfriend and future wife.

Following boot camp, I was granted 2 weeks leave and went to Detroit to be with my parents and friends including my girlfriend. It was great to be home again and see my family that I really missed.

Following my leave I attended a very interesting, five month Hospital Corps School course at the US Naval Hospital always at Great Lakes, Illinois. I found the Hospital Corpsman course very interesting and informative and I really enjoyed learning so many new and interesting medical related skills, like taking body temperature, blood pressures, caring for dying patients, drawing blood, suturing wounds, providing first aid, etc. I was very proud of successfully completing this very interesting five month course and upon graduation I became a proud US Navy Hospital Corpsman and following graduation I received my Hospital Corps graduation certificate and had a great picture taken with the graduating class.

I was granted some leave prior to reporting to my first assignment. While on leave, I also attended my sister's wedding. I was anxious to put these new and important skills to the test. My first duty station was the US Naval Hospital at Newport, RI working in the Sick Officers (SOQ) ward. It was a great experience and I really enjoyed taking care of these interesting patients, mostly WWII veterans who always had interesting war stories to tell, especially their adventures in Italy knowing I was of Italian origins. They appreciated very much the care they received and they let me know it. I was very proud and enjoyed serving these real war heroes.

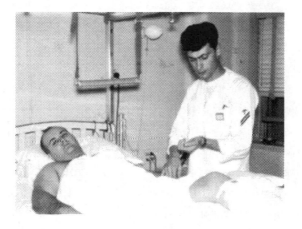

At that time the Red Cross visited the patients weekly and, in addition to other goodies, each patient was given a pack of cigarettes, if I remember correctly they were usually Camels. Since at that time I smoked, many of the kind officers gifted me their pack of cigarettes. One of the patients I cared for was a retired US Navy Four Star admiral who often let me know how much he appreciated the care I provided him. I was surprised and pleased that after he was discharged he and his wife invited me and my wife to their house for dinner. We did not own a car at the time so he sent his driver to pick us up. What an honor for a young, very low ranking enlisted man and his young wife to be invited to the home of an admiral with servants serving dinner and we were treated more like friends. It was an experience which I appreciated and my wife and I will never forget it.

I then worked in the hospital delivery room and nursery which I found very interesting and learned a lot. For the first time in my life I witnessed the live birth of a baby, I was very impressed. I then was assigned to care for aging and very sick patients where I assisted someone who was dying and who died in my arms and

I also witnessed an autopsy for the first time. All interesting new events for me. While at Newport I also took and passed the High School equivalency test and earned a high school certificate. For all practical purposes, I was now a proud High School graduate, which later allowed me to pursue and receive a college degree with the University of Maryland.

As noted above I was stationed at the Newport Naval Hospital where I married Patricia at the hospital chapel where we had only a few friends present but no relatives. However, the first time we returned to Detroit, a few months later, my mother threw a very nice party attended by my relatives and many friends. My Uncle Leo, the one who took me to see the Giro d'Italia in San Marino, as discussed above, was a great chef and prepared an outstanding meal for our party. It was a very nice reception which we very much appreciated, especially the gifts, and we let my parents and uncle know.

In Newport we were offered military base housing which was not fancy but comfortable and safe. During this assignment my first beautiful daughter, Eva Marie was born at the Naval Hospital in Newport where I was assigned.

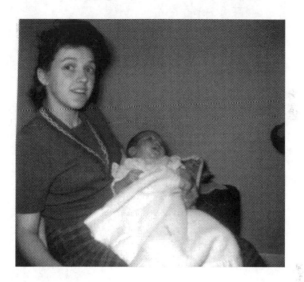

After more than a year a very interesting and educational experience at the Newport Naval Hospital, where I acquired many medical related skills, I applied and was accepted to attend the one year course in X-Ray Technology at the US Naval Hospital at Chelsea, Mass near Boston. Following graduation from X-Ray school, I took and passed the state registry exam and became a proud, state registered X-Ray Technologist. When I reported to Chelsea I was the most junior and lowest ranking student in the class and was made responsible to make the coffee every morning and keep the kitchen clean and in order. Thankfully, after 6 month I was no longer the most junior student and, as a result, I was relived of those extra duties. The school was a combination of classes and on the job training. It was a very interesting one year course where I had the opportunity to learn many new skills and work with Radiologists and experienced X-Ray technicians. I have included a picture of me with a senior student and my very best friend, Rufus giving me tips and learning x-ray techniques.

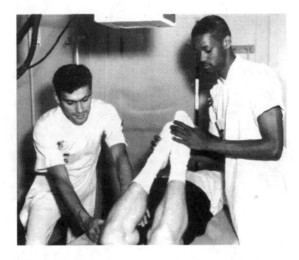

Rufus and I, in addition to working together, we became good friends attended many Boston Red Socks baseball home games and always had great time together. He was and remains great friend for sure. Rufus, like me, is now retired but he is a very skilled and successful nature photographer and, unlike me, he still works. I enjoy seeing his great pictures on the internet. We remain in contact and I hope to meet up again in the future. While stationed in Chelsea, my second beautiful daughter, Jacqueline Domenica was born at the Chelsea Naval Hospital.

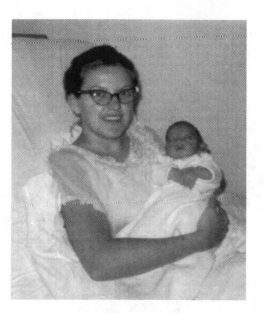

Following this training, and graduation, I was reassigned to the US Naval Hospital in Newport, RI, X-Ray department. I found it very challenging and I really enjoyed putting into practice all I learned at Chelsea and also trained other Corpsmen on X-Ray techniques. My family and I really enjoyed living in Newport with our two daughters. While stationed at the US Naval Hospital in Newport I discussed with a senior Navy chief my immigrating to the US from San Marino at age 11 and how I really missed my native country and all my relatives and friends who live there and would give anything to visit Italy, where San Marino is located. Of course, being a low-ranking enlisted sailor with a wife and two small children I could never afford the trip and would probably never be able to visit and was resigned to this fact. Then one day the kind chief, who served in Italy during the war, called me in his office and asked me if I would be interested in going to a recently established US Navy base in Italy, more specifically, on the Island of Sicily. He informed me they needed an X-Ray Technician and, if I reenlisted, he could arrange for me to get orders to the US

Naval Air Facility (NAF) at Sigonella, Sicily. Of course, I jumped
at the chance, I then reenlisted and soon received orders to report
to the NAF Sigonella. I have included my re-enlistment picture
when I still had hair.

Chapter 7

Being from San Marino, located in Northern Italy, I had never been in southern Italy or the island of Sicily, the most southern part of Italy and was looking forward to serving and living there. Sicily is the biggest and very historic island in the Mediterranean and is beautiful with several much smaller and equally beautiful islands, surrounding the main island. They are the Aeolian Archipelago islands and other small islands like Lampedusa, Egadi, Pelagie, Pantelleria and Ustica. I will discuss these beautiful islands in detail below. The Aeolians Islands are one of 55 UNESCO World Heritage sites in Italy. The island of Sicily has a very interesting history and is peppered with many archaeological sites and a major active volcano, Mt Etna. This is a picture of an erupting Mt Etna which I took shortly after my arrival at Naval Air Station Sigonella.

Mt Etna is a very active volcano and we had a front row seat to witness many eruptions while living there. We also visited some of the active craters a short time after eruptions and found the hardened lava was still warm even several days after the eruption had ceased and the lava had hardened.

The Naval Air Station Sigonella, especially the airfield, has over the years been subject to seasonal severe storms causing the Dittaino River to crest and flood a large land area. The location of Naval Air Station military airport or NAS II is on the low-lying, flat Plain of Catania, ideal for an airfield, but frequently, with the September through December rainy season, there's a good chance of localized flooding. When the flooding occurs, in some cases, families living on and near the installation and the housing area near NAS II have been ordered to boil their water. As a result of some storms, on some occasions the housing residents were evacuated. Sigonella's first major flood occurred mid-September 1959 when the Dittaino Bridge, close NAF II was under six feet of water. As a result of the flood, after 20 September all traffic from the administrative base or NAF I to NAF II airfield was kept to a minimum and vehicles were required to take a circuitous route and go through the city Catania to get to the airfield. Several floods happened over the years after the 1959 flood. In 1964, when I was on active duty serving as a Hospital Corpsman, I took part in rescuing individuals who had been swept out in their automobiles by rushing water. We also assisted in evacuating families from flooded homes. One major flood happened in December 2005 when over 400 service members and their families had to be evacuated from the housing area close to NAS II. In 2006, a newly installed protective barrier prevented a second consecutive year of serious flooding.

The beautiful and historic island of Sicily: Sicily was inhabited more than 10,000 years ago. Its strategic location at the center of the Mediterranean has made the island a crossroads of history, a pawn of conquest and empire, and a melting pot for a dozen or more ethnic groups whose warriors or merchants sought to conquer its shores. Brief history of Sicily: 750 - 215 BC the Greeks govern most of Sicily. In 211 BC the Romans defeat the Greeks at Siracusa, thus bringing to an end nearly 500 years of Sicily's role at the center of Magna Graecia. 468 BC Vandals (of Germanic origin) invade from North Africa and oust the Romans. 476 BC the Ostrogoths ruled Sicily then in 535 – 827 AD the Byzantines ruled, and in 827 – 1061 AD the Arabs ruled, 1060 – in 1194 AD the Normans took over. Sicily is the largest island in the Mediterranean and only dived from mainland Italy by the Strait of Messina, a narrow, 3 km (2 miles) strait between the eastern tip of Sicily (Punta del Faro) and the western tip of Calabria (Punta Pezzo). For many years the construction of a bridge has been discussed and many designs submitted but to date, there is no bridge and ferry boats continue to be utilized for automobiles and trains.

More than 85% of the island is made of hills and mountains. There are very few plains in Sicily, and they make for only 14% of the island terrain. We lived on the largest flat area of Sicily near the city of Catania and near the tallest and most active volcano in Europe, Mount Etna – 3,326 meters or 10,912 feet. There are also several other volcanoes on the island but only two, in addition to Mt Etna, on the main island, are currently active, Stromboli and Vulcano, located on small islands north of the main island. The name Sicily comes from the triangular shape of Sicily, surrounded by 3 different seas: the Mediterranean Sea in the south, Tyrrhenian Sea in the north, Ionian Sea in the east. The old name of Sicily was Trinacria, from the Greek word Τρινακρία, which means "having 3 headlands", or 3 capes. The 3 capes are Peloro (northeast), Passero (south) and Lilbeo (west). For over 2,500 years Sicily, as the strategic crossroads of the western world, left it with an unparalleled historical legacy. Nowhere else have Phoenicians, Greeks, Romans, Byzantines, Arabs, Normans, French, Germans, Spanish, Italians and even the British left such an indelible impression. Whether you are more attracted by Greek temples, Roman villas and aqueducts, Norman cathedrals or Baroque churches, Sicily offers a range of historical sites that are not easily matched anywhere in the world. In ancient times, the island was home to the Greek civilization and, as a result, there are plenty of Greek ruins all over Sicily. The most impressive ancient site is undoubtedly the Valley of the Temples, located in city of Agrigento. In the valley there are a total of 8 Greek Temples, built from 510 BC to 430 BC. In total, there are 9 Greek archeological sites on the island, as discussed as shown in attached pictures. In addition to these, there are over 15 archeological sites from other cultures, like the Sicels, Phoenicians, Romans and Arabs. Despite its largely neglected status, Sicily was able to make meaningful contributions to Roman culture through the historian Diodorus Siculus and the poet Calpurnius Siculus. The most famous archeological remains of this period are the beautiful mosaics of a nobleman's villa in present-day Piazza Armerina as discussed in detail below.

Sicily has its own unique language (or dialect). While Italian is the official language of Sicily and is the only language taught in school, most Sicilians also speak another language, the Sicilian dialect that is considered as a distinct language, and has been recognized as such by the UNESCO. The language has origins from a wide variety of other languages: Latin, Greek, Spanish, French, Catalan, Provençal and Arabic. Most Sicilians converse in Sicilian dialect. Although I understand very little Sicilian, I enjoyed listening to Sicilians speak their dialect while living in Sicily. I do know a few of the most common Sicilian dialect words. Sicily first got its independence in 1071 when Norman adventurer Robert Guiscard conquered the island and displaced the Muslims and he founded the province of Sicily. In 1130, Roger II of Sicily founded the Kingdom of Sicily, an independent kingdom that ruled over Sicily until 1816.

Unfortunately the first Mafia in the world is the Sicilian Mafia. In the 19th century, the first Mafia families emerged in Sicily. The Sicilian Mafia, or *Cosa Nostra*, first started as group of men offering protection to other Sicilians, or retrieving their stolen goods & cattle from thieves. It quickly evolved to a protection racketeering business where locals, who could afford it, were forced to pay for protection by the Mafia; if they failed to pay, the Mafia itself would come after them. Although the Sicilian mafia is the first mafia, but there are now many other mafias in Italy, mostly in Southern Italy and even in the USA. Mussolini had practically eliminated the mafia in Italy but, following the end of World War two and the end of fascism, the mafia re-emerged and some mafia capos who had immigrated to the US returned to Sicily. Unfortunately the mafia is very much present to this day.

The reunification of Italy began in Sicily and Sicily was one of the first territories to merge with other kingdoms which started the reunification of Italy. The Kingdom of the Two Sicily's was created in 1816, when the Kingdom of Sicily merged with the Kingdom of Naples. In 1861, thanks to Giuseppe Garibaldi and his men, the Kingdom of Italy was declared, uniting all of the various regions with the exceptions of the Vatican and my native country of San Marino which remained and remains independent to this day.

The Sicilian soil, because of the volcanic material on the island, is very fertile and also, thanks to the mild climate of Sicily, two crops a year can be cultivated and harvested. The Sicilian streets are lined with good things to eat, for the frugal the best things to eat aren't generally offered by celebrity chefs, the best of Sicilian cuisine, in my opinion, is found in street food, trattorias, and in markets. It is reported that Plato observed: *"Sicilians build things like they will live forever and eat like they will die tomorrow."* And although you might not have thought about it, Sicilian wine is also very good, especially in the western part of Sicily. The Ionians were the first Greeks to establish a permanent presence in Sicily. They encountered an Italic society, the Siceis, hence the Greek name for the island, Sikelia. A group arrived to found Naxos on the sea (below what is now Taormina) around 735 BC. Naxos is believed to be the first permanent Greek settlement in Sicily. Beginning in 800 BC, following several centuries of sporadic contact with Sicily's smaller islands and coastal areas, the Greeks began what is now considered the first mass colonization of Sicily as well as the southern peninsula (what is now Calabria and Puglia) of Italy. As Magna Graecia (Megara Hellas), this region eventually became home to more Greeks than in Greece itself. Within a few centuries, the Greeks completely assimilated the native Sicanians, Sicels, and Elymians and challenging the Carthaginians for control of the island; however, Greek cities often also fought among themselves. The rivalry between Athens and Sparta was infamous. In fact, the major Greek cities often located on the island of Sicily were founded by populations from various cities in Greece. The Greek language, whose alphabet was based on Phoenicians, was the vernacular tongue of Sicily well into the early middle ages. Following many years of Arab influence, Sicily was inhabited by a mix of Christians, Arab Muslims, and Muslim converts at the time of its conquest by the Christian Normans. Arab Sicily had a thriving trade network with the Mediterranean world, and was known in the Arab world as a luxurious and decadent place. The Norman conquest of Sicily began in 1061when Roger de Hauteville and his brother Robert de Guiscard crossed the Straight of Messina from Calabria on the mainland. With only a handful of men they seized Messina. Thirty years later they had driven out the Saracens and were in control of the entire island of Sicily. The Normans, under Robert and Roger, came intending to conquer and the Pope had conferred on Robert the title of "Duke of Sicily", encouraging him to seize the island from the Saracens. Roger crossed the strait first, landing unseen overnight and surprising the Saracen army early in the morning. When Robert's troops landed later that day, they found themselves unopposed since Messina had been abandoned. Robert immediately fortified the city than moved on to Castrogiovanni that is the modern Enna, the strongest fortress in central Sicily. Although the garrison was defeated, the citadel did not fall and Robert returned to Apulia. However, before leaving, he built a fortress at San Marco d'Alunzio, the first of many Norman castles in Sicily. Robert returned in late 1061 and in June 1063 defeated a Muslim army at the Battle of Cerami, securing the Norman foothold on the island. In August 1071, the Normans began a second and successful siege of Palermo and the city of was entered by the Normans on 7 January 1072 and the defenders of the inner-city surrendered. The island was then partitioned with Robert retaining Palermo, half of Messina, and the largely Christian Val Demone, leaving the rest, including what was not yet conquered by the Romans, to Roger. In 1077 Roger besieged Trapani one of the two remaining Saracen strongholds in the west of the island. His son, Jordan, led a sortie which surprised guards of the garrison's livestock. With its food supply cut off, the city soon surrendered. In 1079 Taormina was besieged, and in 1081, in another surprise attack, Jordan, Robert de Sourval and Elias Cartomi conquered, my very favorite city in Sicily, Catania. Where we lived for 12 years, a holding of the emir of Siracusa. Jordan, whom he had left in charge, revolted, forcing him to return to Sicily and subjugate his son. In 1085 he was finally able to undertake a systematic campaign. On 22 May Roger approached Siracusa by sea, while Jordan led a small cavalry detachment 25 kilometers (15 miles) north of the city. On 25 May, the navies of the count and the emir engaged in the harbor, where the latter was killed, while Jordan's forces besieged the city. The siege lasted throughout the summer and when the city capitulated in March 1086, only Noto was still under Saracen dominion. In February 1091 Noto yielded as well, and the conquest of Sicily was complete. In 1130, the territories in southern Italy united as the Kingdom of Sicily, which included the island of Sicily.

Chapter 8

The Norman Rulers in Sicily, Roger I (c. ...Roger II 1095–1154) Simon of Hauteville (1093–1105) Simone D'Altavilla (in Italian). William I (1131–1166), also known as William the Bad or the Wicked. William II (1155–1189), also known as William the Good.

My young wife and I were very excited to get the opportunity to live in Italy and explore Sicily and also be able to visit and introduce to Pat and my daughters my relatives in San Marino.

As noted above, Sicily is a very historic, beautiful and a most interesting part of modern day Italy and is Italy's largest island. We had the pleasure of living in this beautiful island for 12 wonderful years. Sicilians, especially a few years ago but even to this day, have beautiful decorations of their horses and carts as showed in one of the pictures.

Following two weeks leave to visit our families in Detroit, in December 1963 I departed for Sicily with, for me, an interesting stopover of one day in Rome, where I had never visited. The next day I flew to Catania and was picked up at the airport by my sponsor, and taken to the base. The next day I reported for duty at the medical dispensary at NAF, now NSA Sigonella. The base is about 10 miles distance from Catania the second largest city in Sicily, and is located in one of the rare flat areas on the island. The large city is surrounded by orange, lemon and tangerine orchards as well as many other agriculture fields. The weather, being moderate, allows farmers in Sicily to grow and harvest two crops a year. The tangerines and oranges are delicious, especially the red "blood" oranges. Once I reported to the Medical dispensary at Sigonella, I requested a couple of days leave in order to visit my relatives in my native San Marino that I had not seen for more than 10 years. A kind supervisor, a US Navy Chief, approved and I was granted the leave and took an overnight train to Rimini then a bus from Rimini to San Marino. I was overjoyed to visit with all my close relatives, like my grandfather, uncles, aunts, many cousins, and also old friends that I had not seen for many years. It was a short 4 day but wonderful visit. I have attached a picture of me in San Marino with my grandfather Cristofero.

I returned to Sicily and a week later my wife and daughters arrived. For my wife, who had never been outside the United States, it was quite a change and a great experience. We had a great sponsor who took care of reserving hotel rooms and took us to a very nice hotel, the Hotel Costa in Catania. We stayed at the hotel while waiting for our furniture and automobile. Once settled in the hotel, we had the opportunity to visit the beautiful city of Catania, at times in a horse and buggy which my daughters loved. We also experienced eating great Italian and Sicilian food in some outstanding Trattorias and restaurants in the area. When we arrived in Sicily in 1963 the Sicilian society was at that time very traditional (old fashioned). Widows dressed in black with head covering (looked more like practicing Muslim women than Italian) and young girls were not allowed to leave the house alone or to date unless escorted by a close adult family member, usually male. For this reason, I believe, many Sicilian girls at that time married very young. It was an interesting experience, especially for an American family, to live in a traditional and complex society and culture. We were nonetheless very happy to have the opportunity to live in this unique part of Italy. Once our automobile, a large 1956 Chevrolet, arrived we had the opportunity to begin searching for an apartment to rent. This was 1963 when almost all automobiles in Sicily were Fiat 500's, very small cars and there weren't very many since most Sicilians did not own a car. Our 1956 Chevrolet was twice the size of a Fiat 500 and, of course, we always attracted a crowd wherever we went.

1956 Chevrolet Bel Air

The other mode of transportation in Sicily at the time were scooters, and my girls wanted to try sitting on one and I took a picture.

Most Americans working at the base, while waiting to be assigned American style family housing on the military base, they rented apartments in the large city of Catania, about 10 miles from the base. From where I worked on the base I could see a little town on a hill with a large, what I found out later was a Norman castle, only a couple of miles away.

I inquired about the town, but no one was familiar with this town named Motta Sant Anastasia since it was not located on the main road to Catania and I couldn't find anyone who had even driven through there. Motta San Anastasia, a charming small town with Greek origins dating back to the 4th – 5th century BC. The town is rich in *history* and in incredible cultural attractions such as its Mother Church and its Norman *Castle*. The castle was built by the Normans around 1080 on behalf of Roger I, King of Sicily. In 1091, the castle it was granted to the Bishop of Catania and in 1250 it was taken from the Bishop by Frederick II, Holy Roman Emperor. In 1267 it went to the Capetian House of Anjou, and was later conquered by the Romans. The role of the castle grew in the Middle Ages during the *Norman* period and, for four centuries until the 20th century, the *castle* was used as a prison.

Rumors on the base were that the citizens of the town were not very friendly and possibly anti–American – which was, as I discovered, far from the truth. Motta Sant Anastasia, is an agricultural town with a population, at the time, of less than 6000 mostly hard working farmers. I was curious and one day decided to visit. When we arrived in the main square of the town, our large automobile attracted attention and we were surrounded by many curious locals who had never seen an automobile as big as ours. My wife was alarmed and wanted to leave when a very nice gentleman approached the car and introduced himself as Carmelo Schillagi and we had a nice conversation. He then invited us to visit his nearby home, which we happily accepted. We met his wife Filomena and two children, Santina and Pino. Attached is a picture of Filomena and Carmelo when they were married and a picture of them when we first met them holding my daughter Eva.

They were so kind that my wife and daughters, although not understanding the language, felt right at home. They had us over for a great Italian lunch and we had a wonderful day. I mentioned to Carmelo that we were looking for an apartment and would be interested in moving to Motta if I could find an adequate apartment to rent. He promised to look around and help us find a suitable one. No other American had even visited Motta let alone look for an apartment there. A week later we returned to Motta and Carmelo took us to an apartment that was available to rent. It was a brand new and we found it to be very nice and decided to rent it, signed a rental contract and made arrangements to move in. It was a pleasant apartment with a great view of the Sicilian countryside; however, like all apartments in this town it did not have central heating. Fortunately winters in Sicily are of short duration with mostly mild temperature. The only problem was the dampness that could get uncomfortable. We purchased a kerosene space heater and also had a wood burning stove (like the one I had as a child in San Marino) which provided adequate heat. Once our furniture arrived we had it delivered and the curious locals were impressed by the American size refrigerator, more than twice the size of typical Italian refrigerators and the TV which very few Sicilians at the time had in their homes. However, soon after we moved in we were considered part of the town. Everyone, especially Filomena, Carmelo and family looked out for us and assisted my wife, who could not speak Italian, in finding her way around town. Filomena escorted Pat to grocery stores and warned the owners to treat her right and not to overcharge her. Being the town's only mid wife, Filomena had delivered most babies in Motta for 20 years, she was therefore respected and her word meant a lot. Since Pat was not familiar with the local currency, the store owners agreed to keep a running tab that I would pay every Saturday and it worked out well. We were treated with a lot of respect and kindness, which my family really appreciated. We made many friends in the town, including some Italian military. At that time, all men were required to serve unless they had a medical or other reasons to request an exception. Attached is a picture of me in uniform with my friend and Motta neighbor, Salvatore who was at the time serving in the Italian Army.

While serving at Sigonella on my first tour I met Joan Crawford when she visited NAF Sigonella with a USO show. She was at the time well-known American actress who started as a dancer in traveling theatrical companies before debuting on Broadway. She was active from 1924 to 1974. It was a pleasure, for a young enlisted sailor to meet such, at the time, a famous actress and I found her to be a very nice person who was kind enough to take a picture with me.

Our daughter Eva began going to Italian pre-school (asilo★/) and, although Jackie was not old enough and not potty trained, she really wanted to join her sister. We made a deal with her that she could join her sister once she was totally potty trained and the teacher agreed. She was soon potty trained and the teacher agreed for her to join her sister in asilo. They both did very well and were soon speaking enough Italian to converse with the teacher and the other children. My two little ones were just super cute and smart; everyone in the town loved them. Attached are some pictures of them the first two years we lived in Motta. My girls really enjoyed that wonderful little town and the folks in Motta loved my girls, especially Filomena who made sure she would arranged to celebrate their birthday. The girls enjoyed getting together with the Schillagi family, as shown in some of these pictures.

My wife was also learning basic (survival) Italian. What was interesting was the fact that no one in this little town had a home phone, there was only one telephone in the town, a public phone, located in the city hall and that was the only way one could be contacted via telephone. If a call came in for us, a messenger would come to the house with a message. Then we could go to city hall during working hours to return the call or make other phone calls for a fee and it worked well. My girls were doing well in asilo and my wife, with the loving help of Filomena and other Italian ladies in the town, was learning and speaking basic Italian and learned how to get around this little wonderful town, doing shopping and making other friends. She also spent time with a seamstress and learned the basics of sewing and tailoring and also practiced her Italian. The folks in Motta were outstanding, just good friendly, loving people and we made many life-long friends. We could not have asked for better friends. We moved very close to Filomena, Carmelo and their family and spent a lot of time together. Carmelo and Filomena had two children, Pino and Santina who became very close to us, especially Santina.

A few years after we moved to Motta, Santina was married and she moved on the floor above her parents and close to us. We were very close to her and she, like her mom became a mid-wife. Living in Motta Sant Anastasia was a wonderful experience for me and my family. Things were also going pretty well for me at work. I had my own little, one man X-Ray department and I really enjoyed it. Other Corpsmen assisted me and I trained some to take basic X-rays. The small Sigonella Medical Dispensary was staffed by 14-16 Corpsmen, two doctors, two nurses a Dentist and Dental technician. That being the case, in addition to our primary assigned duties, we were all expected to perform other functions, like laboratory work, giving shots, suturing, etc. Two Corpsmen, one senior and one junior, were on duty in the dispensary after normal working hours and were expected handle all medical care, including driving an ambulance to respond to emergencies such as car accidents. I sutured many cuts and even once did a tracheotomy and a temporary dental filling – it was very challenging and interesting experience and I really enjoyed the job and all the challenges. Although we lived off the base we maintained our connection to the American community by doing some of our shopping at the Base Exchange and taking part in American activities and having some American friends. At Christmas we took our kids to meet Santa who had arrived in a military aircraft at the NSA Sigonella military airfield. They really enjoyed meeting Santa and as can be seen in the picture with Santa holding Eva while Jackie looks on. These activities ensured the girls maintained their connection to the US.

Soon after we moved to Motta my wife became pregnant for the third time and the girls were excited for the upcoming addition to the family. Due to some previous health issues, my wife was admitted to the US Naval Hospital in Naples, 250 miles from where we lived, for observation for almost two months from the anticipated delivery date. I worked full time with duty nights and was now also totally responsible for the care for two very young daughters. Fortunately, in addition to the Schillagi family, we had a great neighbor, Donna Marta, who agreed to assist me in taking care of the girls.

They spent the day with her and she took such good care of them they usually wanted to spend the night with her rather than come home with me, they really loved this great lady, and I did, too. I will always be indebted to her for the care she took of my girls. I have included a picture of Donna Marta. We also spent a lot of time and had meals with the Schillagi family. This time my wife delivered a beautiful baby boy and we now had a son in addition to our two wonderful daughters and the girls were thrilled to have a little brother. We named him Anthony Lester to honor my father as well as Pat's father. We had him baptized in the main Motta church with Filomena and Carmelo as the proud God parents. It was a very nice ceremony followed by a small party for our friends from Motta and the Sigonella base. Attached are pictures of the baptism and of the godmother, Filomena taken soon after the baptism and a picture of my family, including Anthony.

Things were busy with three small children at home but with the help and love of Donna Marta, Filomena and family we did well. As noted above, we were the first American family to live in Motta but soon after we settled there other Americans began looking for and renting apartments in Motta where the rents were cheaper than in the big city of Catania and it was so much closer to the base. I was happy that some Americans moved to Motta because it really helped the local economy with additional construction jobs and supporting the local merchants. The girls were also doing well at the asilo and really enjoyed it and began speaking Italian with ease and interpreted for their mother, although Pat's Italian was also, although slowly, coming along well. The girls, as young as they were, also interpreted for other Americans who had moved to Motta. As time went by we became closer to Filomena, Carmelo and family and other folks in town and took part in local festivities and functions, such as Carnevale (Mardi gras) and the feast of the Patron Saint, Anastasia, etc. We introduced some of our American friends, including my best friend and fellow corpsman, Russ Brown to the town and all of our Sicilian friends. Russ became a friend with many folks in Motta. Russ at the time was single and he frequently dined with us and the Schillagi family.

Big Russ, who was over 6 feet tall, and stocky stood out since most Sicilians men were not very tall and were generally thin. I would like to add that I worked with Russ at the Sigonella dispensary when he was assigned to assist me in taking X-Rays. I trained him and urged Russ to become a Hospital Corpsman, which he did. He was so successful that he later was commissioned as a Medical Service Corps (MSC) Officer attaining the rank of Captain, an amazing career. Russ was a very good person who was very kind and I really admired him. A few years ago we visited him and his wife in Florida as shown in attached picture.

I recently received the very sad news that Russ passed away in 2021, my family and I lost a dear friend. Russ and other military from Sigonella played on a basketball team and offered to play an Italian team from Motta. I made the arrangement and a makeshift basketball court was set up a in the main town square (or piazza). The games were a big hit attended by most of the folks living in Motta and they enjoyed the games although the Italian team lost most of the time. We enjoyed living in Motta so much that we turned down American style base housing, with all the modern conveniences, including central heat and air conditioning, when it was offered, preferring to continue living the Italian experience on the Motta economy. Things were also going well at work and I enjoyed the challenges and really learned a lot. I frequently drove the ambulance to react to emergencies. I handled, in some cases, all kinds of serious emergencies, including assisting a birth and enjoyed the challenges of the job. Life for me and my family was good. For starters we loved living in Motta, plus the cost of living in Sicily at that time was very reasonable as compared to the US where we struggled to live on the salary of low raking enlisted person. In the states I always had a second or third part time jobs to supplement my income. In Sicily my pay was more than enough to live well. Also we enjoyed frequently visiting my native country of San Marino_and my relatives were thrilled to spend time with us and our children. As I said, things were going well until one day our little boy Anthony became very ill. We took him to the base dispensary where he was admitted. Sadly he died that night on what appeared to be "sudden infant death syndrome". It was tragic for Pat and me but especially hard on the girls who loved their little brother and could not understand what happened. Our families in the states were also devastated and very sorry they never even got to meet Anthony. We made the decision to bury him in the cemetery in my birth town of Domagnano in San Marino. The

US Navy was very supportive and provided a US Navy airplane to take us with the casket to San Marino.

The folks in Motta, especially Filomena, Carmelo and family, were heart broken and provided as much support as possible as did our American friends on the base, especially Russ. All my relatives and many of our friends came to the funeral service and the cemetery. Following the funeral we returned to Sicily and did our very best to carry on but it was not easy. Fortunately we had the love and support of Filomena, Carmelo and family as well as other Italian and American friends and that helped us cope and I will be forever grateful. In Nov1965 I received orders to report to the USS Bushnell AS-15, homeported in Key West, FL. On 5 Dec 1965 we departed Sigonella in our VW Bug on our way Naples, Italy.

In Naples we boarded the ship the SS Constitution with our car for a very interesting 12 day trip back to the states. The SS Constitution, over the years, had many celebrity passengers. For example on April 4 1956, Grace Kelly and fifty of her family, bridesmaids and her poodle boarded the SS Constitution at New York's Pier 84 for her voyage to her prince and new homeland Monaco. In addition, it is said she had over eighty pieces of luggage. Even though 400 reporters applied to sail on this voyage the vast majority were turned away and only a few were permitted to board the ship. Thousands of people saw the ship off as she sailed for eight days across the Atlantic to Monaco where the ship had to anchor just outside the harbor. Prince Rainer's yacht, the "Deo Juvante" was sent out to the ship to bring Grace ashore. As Grace Kelly stepped ashore from Rainier's yacht, well over 20,000 locals and tourists were there to welcome her to Monaco. Eight days later Prince Rainier the third and Grace Patricia Kelly were married in a civil ceremony in the throne room at the Palace in Monaco, which was a requirement by the law of the land. However, the very next day the grand ceremonial wedding took place in the Monaco Cathedral.

On our 12 day trip we experienced several days of rough seas, after all it was winter. Pat and Eva were often sea sick and skipped some meals, but it did not bother Jackie and me and we continued to eat all of our meals. The girls really enjoyed the trip with all 4 of us sleeping in bunk beds in the same cabin. Every night I received a good night kiss from my two beautiful daughters. I've enclosed a pictures of the girls kissing me good night and the family on board the ship.

We arrived in New York City on a cold December day I will never forget seeing the Statue of Liberty for the second time in my life, the first time was in 1952 when we immigrated to the US. I was nonetheless impressed. We retrieved our car and luggage and drove to Detroit. When we arrived, we found Detroit to be cold and snow covered and it was an enjoyable novelty for the girls since it never snowed where we lived in Sicily. We had an emotional visit with my parents and other relatives and shared our grief at the loss of Anthony. This is a picture of my girls with their cousin, my sister's daughter, Tina. Notice the matching dresses, a gift from my mother who was very proud of her three granddaughters.

Chapter 9

A fter two weeks leave, in mid Jan 1966, I had an interesting two long days drive from Detroit to Key West, FL in my reliable VW Bug. It was a long but enjoyable drive. Once I arrived in Key West I reported for duty on board the US Navy ship, USS Bushnell AS-15. The ship was a Submarine Tender (provided support to submarines) and it was my one and only ship while serving 10 years in the US Navy.

My family came to Key West as soon as I found an affordable house to rent. It was a nice little house located in a trailer park. An additional benefit was a pay telephone located right outside our house. It was convenient since we could not afford our own phone. Weather wise, it was quite a pleasant change in January weather from Detroit to Key West, FL where we could go swimming.

Enclosed is a picture taken in January 1966 with my girls in our back yard.

I enjoyed working on the ship and dealing with submarine sailors. One day the Commanding Officer of one of the submarines serviced by the USS Bushnell came to see me and asked if I could go out to sea with his submarine for a few days since their Corpsman was under the weather and the submarine could not go out to sea without a qualified Corpsman to take care of possible emergencies out at sea. Since I was qualified for independent duty, I was authorized to serve and provide the required medical support which would allow the submarine to get underway. However, I really was not certain I wanted to go on a small diesel powered submarine on maneuvers even for just a few days. I eventually agreed to go in order to allow the submarine to perform scheduled operations. As it turned out it was for me an exciting and enjoyable three days of participating on maneuvers. Also the food they served was plentiful and great and included lobster. The Commander of the submarine was very grateful I agreed to join them to allow operating and he presented me with an "Honorary Submariner" certificate. I was very happy and honored and to be of help. I was on board the USS Bushnell when in 1965 she suffered a serious fire in some electrical generation equipment - and the ship then and forever earned the nick-name "the Burning Bush". Fortunately there was only one minor injury in that incident, and it didn't effect operations for long. When I heard "fire - fire" on the PA system I assumed, like most of the crew, it was the usual drill until a second message came over the PA that stated "this is not a drill, this is not a drill." We then all went to our assigned battle stations and waited until the all clear was announced. A couple of weeks after the fire, the ship was towed to Charleston, SC shipyard for repair work. We spent a few months in Charleston, and it was quite an experience for me since I had never been in a southern state. Keep in mind this was 1965 and for the first time in my life I experienced segregation and it concerned me since my best friend on the ship was, like me, from Detroit and happened to be African-American. While in Charleston we were very careful where we went. Once we drove together from Charleston to Key West to visit our families and it involved driving through Georgia in addition to South Carolina and Florida. To avoid any problems on the trip, I would purchase take-out food and we ate in the car. The Bushnell returned to its home port in Key West in 1967 to continue her service to submarines.

All of the Corpsmen on the USS Bushnell were either coming from or could expect to receive orders to Vietnam, which included me. However, since I was a senior Hospital Corpsman and also X-Ray Technician, I would not be assigned to serve in combat with the US Marines as were most junior Corpsmen. I would most likely be assigned to a hospital ship with an X-Ray room, such as USS Repose off the Vietnam coast. As I was preparing for orders, I received a call from a fellow corpsman and a good friend of mine,

Bill Goodhart, who had been stationed with me at Sigonella and was now at US Navy Headquarters at the Corpsmen assignment desk. He informed me that he could arrange for my return to Sigonella since the X-Ray Technician who had taken my place did not like it there at all and wanted a transfer. Of course I jumped on the chance and soon received orders back to NAS Sigonella.

Chapter 10

On 10 Dec 1966, my family and I took a flight to Catania, Sicily. When we arrived at Fontanarossa, the Catania airport we were greeted by several Sicilian friends who came to welcome us back. It was moving to see so many of our Sicilian friends. Our daughters were thrilled to see so many people who they knew were there to welcome us back. Filomena and Carmelo took us to the Hotel Costa in Catania where we settled down for the night. They came to pick us up almost every day and we spent a lot of time with them and had some great meals. The Schillagi family were and are more like family than simply friends and it seemed like we had never left. Our VW Bug had arrived and we were able to get around town. Since Filomena and Carmelo were Anthony's God parents, we did a little crying together remembering our little son. My friend and Carmelo's brother, Nino Schillagi had an apartment that was free and he could rent to us and we took it and we moved in not long after our arrival. This time it was possible to have a home phone in Motta and we got one. Once we settled down we registered our girls in the local school and, since they knew the language, for them it was an easy transition. Filomena made sure that we had what we needed in the house and helped Pat with the shopping. We spent a lot of time with the Schillagi family and loved it, it was really like coming back home. Also, with the cost of living in Sicily was still reasonable and the fact I had been promoted to HM1 (E-6), we did not have a money problem like we had in the states and it was a great feeling.

We soon settled in our apartment, as noted above, rented to us by my friend Nino Schillagi. Also, as discussed above, we had been the first American military family to move and live in this wonderful little town but I'm happy to report that other American military families followed us to live in Motta and to this day many American military families live there and support the local economy.

Motta Sant Anastasia is a very old and historic town. Information I found on the internet notes that the oldest part of Motta Sant Anastasia was built on a volcanic plug, dating back many years. Over the centuries, through erosion, the cone has acquired its current shape. Archaeological studies found Greek presence in the territory around the 5th–4th centuries BC. The Roman period is evidenced by the discovery of some coins and a mosaic from the period of the great empire. Motta, since as early as the 4th century BC, has held a role of considerable importance as a stronghold of warning and defense. Over the years, Motta belonged to several feudal lords, such as Russo, Perolo, Ruiz de Lihari, and ultimately Moncada, to whom it remained until the abolition of the feudal rights. The most interesting monuments, architecturally speaking, are the Norman Castle, built during the XI century and the Chiesa Madre or main church was built during the XII century. The main church is notable by two domes with semicircular chapels. The chiesa dell'Immacolata, originally known as "chiesa del villaggio", the first building of this church goes back to 1000 AD and the wall was probably built using lava stones. A must see in the church are the five paintings of the seventeenth century. It is reported that there are several hypotheses on the name Sant' Anastasia. According to some scholars Motta (pre-Roman name) and Anastasia (Greek-Byzantine name) have similar meanings and indicate the nature of the place. Later in the 12th–14th centuries, the two names were combined and citizens joined in devotion and worship of Saint

Anastasia, who is considered the patron saint of the town. During the Norman rule, Count Roger of Hauteville built a tower in basalt stone to guard the entrance to the plains of Catania and protect the area from Saracen incursions. The tower was built by the Normans between 1070 and 1074 AD. The massive tower with a base of about 21.5 by 9 by 17 meters is about 21 meters tall and is a typical defensive structure of the early middle Ages. As shown in attached picture. In 1526 AD the city became a fief of Antonio Moncada, Count of Adernò and for four centuries, until the 20th century, the castle was used as a prison. In the late 17th century there were 560 inhabitants in Motta. In 1798 the inhabitants of Motta became 1400, rising to 2181 in the 1831 census. The population when we lived there was approximately 6000 and the current population is approximately 12,000, which includes several American families.

On 1 January 1820 the Court of Catania founded the separate town/commune of Motta Sant' Anastasia. Motta is a wonderful little town with so many, wonderful and hardworking people who lived a simple life. When we moved there in 1963 not all homes had running water and many folks used the public fountains like this beautiful lady whose picture I took.

I reported to the NAS Sigonella base and began working at my old X-Ray area and doing other functions at the dispensary as I had done in the past. Like when I was there the first time, the dispensary had a staff of 14-16 Corpsmen, two doctors, two nurses, a dentist and Dental Technician. I was now one of the most senior and an experienced corpsman and I did my best to help the younger corpsmen and I enjoyed very much working with them. As noted above, the corpsmen took care of all the emergency care as well as routine sick call. The doctors were available as needed however; after normal working hours and weekends the corpsmen on duty took care of all minor injuries and provided first aid, like suturing, etc. We all drove the ambulance and responded to automobile accidents and other emergencies anywhere on the island, as needed. We also took care of handling and preparing deceased personnel for movement to the Naval Hospital in Naples for embalming and return the remains to the United States. It was not a very pleasant task, but someone had to do it. And since I was one of the most senior and experienced corpsman, I often accompanied patients from Sigonella to the Naval Hospital in Naples. The patients were usually transported to Naples Naval Hospital on military flights. At that time the military plane utilized was a vintage C-130 prop plane. On one typical, normal two hour flight which was usually pretty routine except this one time when I was caring for a severely injured patient, involved in a serious automobile accident. When we approached Capodichino, the Naples airport, the airplane experienced mechanical problems and had to make an emergency landing. We had a very rough landing and went off the runway but we made it without any injuries, just a little shook up. Normally that type of emergency landing would have me concerned or even scared but since I was concentrating on taking care of the seriously injured patient and felt responsible of keeping him calm and ensure his safety, I did not give the emergency landing much of a thought.

It was an exciting trip, the patient did well and I was very happy to return home to Sigonella the following day.

While I was serving as a Hospital Corpsman at Sigonella I took part in providing medical assistance to individuals out at sea. I would be transported by helicopter and lowered to the place where the individual requiring medical care was located. I provided first aid and, when necessary, assisted in transporting the patient to a medical facility.

The medical dispensary at Sigonella was responsible for providing emergency medical care for military and civilian personnel stationed at the US military facilities in Sigonella and other locations on the island, as required. Most emergencies were as a result of automobile accidents and an ambulance would be dispatched to provide first aid and transportation to the Sigonella dispensary or a local Italian hospital. As one of the senior corpsmen I often responded to emergencies and determined if we could handle the emergency at the dispensary or a local Italian hospital. If I determined that we couldn't provide the required medical care/assistance locally, the patient would be evacuated via military air to the US Naval hospital in Naples.

My family and I really enjoyed living in this beautiful and historic, quaint little town for many years and having made and still have so many great Sicilian friends who live there. We also became friends with Americans, mostly military, who lived and worked on the base and, as noted above, many moved to Motta once they saw it was safe to live there and be a lot closer to the military base. One of our closest friends who moved to Motta was a US Navy nurse, Terry who with her husband moved next door to us. She was a great nurse, beautiful person and a great friend, very close to my wife.

While having a picnic on a beach with her husband, parents and siblings near Taormina she ran in the sea to assist her younger sister who had been swept out to sea and was having difficulty getting out. Unfortunately she could not get her sister out and she, her sister and an Italian man who had jumped in to help all drowned. They all three disappeared without a trace and their remains were never found. It was, to say the least, a tragic event which affected us deeply, especially my wife who was so close to Terry.

As noted above, the population of Motta when we lived there was an estimated 6000. My girls were again enrolled in the Motta School system, Enclosed is a picture of my daughter Eva's third grade class.

My girls continued to attended Italian school and correctly spoke both Italian and English. In order to have them not lose their English speaking skills and maintain their American identity we had them join the Girl Scouts of America that was active at the Sigonella base. They enjoyed being Girl Scouts and taking part in the activities associated with the scouts. My daughter Eva won first place prize in a Girls Scouts contest with an essay entitled: "why I'm proud to be an American." A copy of the essay and a picture of my girls in the scout uniform are enclosed.

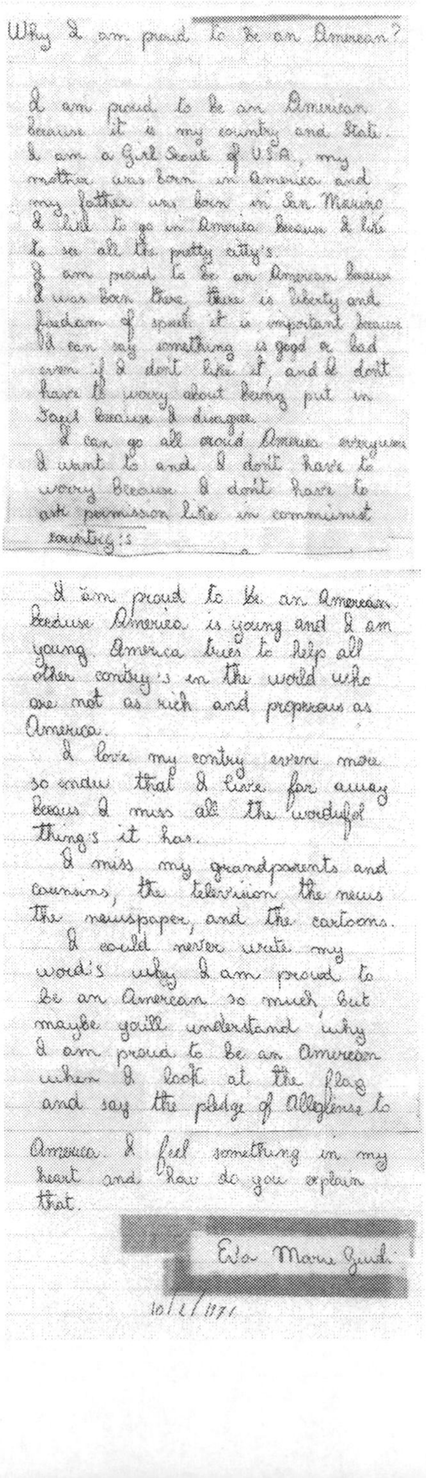

Why I am proud to be an American?

I am proud to be an American because it is my country and state. I am a Girl Scout of USA, my mother was born in America and my father was born in San Mauro. I will to go in America because I like to see all the pretty city's.

I am proud to be an American because I was born there, there is liberty and freedom of speech it is important because I can say something is good or bad even if I don't like it, and I don't have to worry about being put in Jail because I disagree.

I can go all around America everywhere I want to and I don't have to worry because I don't have to ask permission like in communist country's.

I am proud to be an American because America is young and I am young, America tries to help all other country's in the world who are not as rich and properous as America.

I love my country even more so endu that I live far away because I miss all the wonderful thing's it has.

I miss my grandparents and cousins, the television the news the newspaper, and the cartoons.

I could never write my word's why I am proud to be an American so much, but maybe you'll understand why I am proud to be an American when I look at the flag and say the pledge of Allegiance to America I feel something in my heart and how do you explain that.

Eva Marie Guidi

10/2/1171

It was a great essay of a proud American girl living in Sicily, and Jackie's essay came in second. I was very proud of both of my girls, who, although living in Italy, were proud Americans. The Girl Scouts camped out and visited other American bases in Naples and Vicenza for scouting events. They really enjoyed traveling, being scouts and it helped them maintain their American connection. My wife often joined the girls as an adult escort when they traveled to other bases in Italy. Life in Motta was pleasant and my wife became proficient in speaking Italian and enjoyed getting together with other ladies in the town to do basic tailoring and other sewing activities. I enjoyed working at the dispensary and performing a variety of tasks such as suturing wounds, driving the ambulance to respond to emergencies and training junior Corpsmen since I was now the senior corpsman. We could not have asked for a better place to live, raise a family, have better working conditions and many good, sincere friends. Also, my US Navy income was more than sufficient to support the family. I have to say that life was good and we were grateful.

Most Sicilians are traditional Roman Catholics and have many celebrations in honor of saints, especially saints of Sicilian origin. For example, Saint Anastasia is the patron saint of Motta. Saint Agata, who was born in Catania, is the patron saint of that city. She was born in 231 AD and died a martyr on February 5, 251 AD in Catania. She was canonized on 5 Feb in year 600 AD and her feast day is celebrated on that date. For three days, 3-5 Feb of every year, thousands of Catania and other devotees feverishly celebrate the virgin. She is buried in the main cathedral in Catania. Coincidentally, Saint Agata is also the patron saint of San Marino, my birth country. San Marino celebrates their liberation, which took place on 5 February 1740 when cardinal Enriquez, representing the Vatican, returned San Marino's autonomy which cardinal Alberoni, wanting to expand the Papal State's power base in the region, tried to subjugate San Marino. Alberoni invaded

San Marino on October 17th 1739. Unhappy with the aggressive way he was ruling the country and the whole invasion thing, the people of San Marino protested against Alberoni's occupation and appealed directly to the Vatican. Messages were sent to obtain justice from Pope Clemente XII. The Pope recognized the rights of San Marino to be independent and on 5 February 1740 restored the country's independence on Saint Agata's feast day. As part of the celebration to mark Liberation Day and honor Saint Agata, there is a public procession with the statue of the Saint from the city of Borgo Maggiore to the capital city of San Marino. In addition, various civic celebrations take place throughout the day. An image of Saint Agata along with images of San Marino and San Leo is found on the Public Palace of the Republic of San Marino as shown in attached picture.

Legend is that Agata was the beautiful daughter of a wealthy family from port city of Catania that was colonized by the Greeks. A faithful Christian, Agatha swore herself to Christ. Important to know that during her lifetime Christianity was illegal under Roman rule. So, when the strong-willed young woman refused the advances of Quintianus, a Roman prefect, he arrested her on account of her religion. To celebrate their patron saint, Catania's faithful engage in back-breaking activities to illustrate their devotion to their patroness. For example, they pull the extremely heavy "fercolo" through the city streets when the citizens work together, as a community to honor their patron saint. During the festivities there are no barriers, few police, no men on horseback or dogs just a community working and celebrating together and there is a pure sense of fraternity, community, and hope among the "cittadini. The fireworks each night are magnetic and people come in droves to witness them and they also come to light candles as an act of prayer for the saint. As noted above, Saint Agata is also the patron saint of San Marino. On and her feast day, as part of the celebrations to mark San Marino Liberation Day, as noted above, various civic celebrations also take place throughout the day.

While in Sicily we also had some interesting cultural experiences like going to operas. We went several times for operas performed at the beautiful "Teatro Massimo Bellini", the first opera house in Sicily, named on honor of this Catanese composer, is located on the appropriately named Piazza Vincenzo Bellini in Catania. The theater, also named in his honor, was inaugurated in 1890. The Massimo Bellini Theater can be considered the driving force of music life in Catania as well as a Sicilian wonder. It has a capacity of about 1200 seats and perfect acoustics. Norma is the most popular performance of the composer's masterwork. My wife and I and other American friends attended and enjoyed Norma and many other performances in this beautiful theater. In Palermo, the capital of Sicily, there is the Teatro Massimo

Vittorio Emanuele, or simply Teatro Massimo where operas are performed. The building was inspired by ancient and classical Sicilian architecture and thus, the exterior was designed in the high neoclassical style incorporating elements of the Greek temples at Selinunte and Agrigento.

Chapter 11

A fter about a year in my second stint at Sigonella, my younger brother, Marino joined the US Navy and he requested, following completion of boot camp, to be assigned for duty with his brother in Sicily. A request that was approved and soon after boot camp he joined us at Sigonella. The girls were more than delighted to have their uncle come live with us. Fortunately we had an extra bedroom for him to use. Marino was there when the girls were confirmed and received first communion and he took part in the celebration and the girls were thrilled.

Marino quickly familiarized himself with the area and I know he enjoyed his assignment working in the Supply Department at Sigonella as a Store Keeper, and he did well. As opposed to me,

Marino played various sports in high school so he had no problem joining sport teams at the Sigonella base and he did well.

Although he played various sports, his favorites were baseball and ice hockey. Of course he could not play ice hockey in Sicily so he learned to play soccer but concentrated on baseball. He did so well that an Italian semi-professional baseball team recruited him and he became their star player. His favorite position was first base but could play other positions, including pitcher. He was a good left handed pitcher and was often used in that position by his Italian team. However, there was an Italian baseball rule that teams could have a maximum of three foreign players but non-Italian players could not be used to pitch. The first time Marino was brought in to pitch, the opposing team objected to him pitching citing the rule on foreign players. Since Marino, like me, was born in San Marino he was considered to be an Italian player. When he was challenged he pulled out his San Marino passport to prove he was eligible. His team, thanks in part to Marino, made the playoffs and played in various Italian cities, including Rome. I went to Rome to be with Marino and watch him play and we had a good time. It was really great to have my little brother with us. Marino also played soccer with a group of other US military at the base and played at lunch time against a group of Italian employees of the Supply Department, as shown in the attached picture.

Bowling was introduced to Italy in 1965 and a year later a bowling alley was opened in Catania. Since the military base, at the time, did not have a bowling alley, the Catania facility became very popular with Americans stationed at Sigonella and a few bowling teams were formed by Americans from Sigonella. Sicilians were introduced to bowling for the first time and, of course, they had a steep learning curve but they were anxious to learn this new sport and many Americans were kind enough to teach bowling to Sicilians. In 1968 Marino and I joined a bowling team that, considering most of our averages, we were appropriately named "The Handicappers". After an expected last place finish the first year we recruited Carmelo, an Italian/Sicilian who had mastered bowling in a years' time and had a more than decent average. The second year all of us improved a little bit but, with the exception of Carmelo, still had high handicaps to add to our score and Carmelo got even better. We shocked everyone and beat the best team in the finals and finished in first place and won the cup, as can be seen in the pictures and a picture of me congratulating Carmelo for having the best average of the league. It was a lot of fun.

In addition to being a good athlete, Marino was also a good coach and he began coaching the children of the military personnel stationed at Sigonella. He was responsible for putting together the very first Sigonella Little League baseball program. His team did well and played against Little League teams at other US military bases in Italy. It was great for the kids and Marino really enjoyed it. To this day Marino, now in his seventies, still enjoys coaching ice hockey teams in Detroit, including the one his talented grandson plays on, and is very successful. I was and still am very proud of my little brother. After 2 years at Sigonella Marino received orders to report to a ship. We hated to see him leave, especially the girls who loved having their uncle living with us for two years but were grateful we had the opportunity to be together for two years.

While in Sicily we also enjoyed visiting and dining at local restaurants (trattoria) and enjoyed some great, simple, typical Sicilian meals. These establishments are not very fancy, most with a limited selection, but the food was usually great at very reasonable prices. The caption above one of the pictures reads: "Not taking anything away from Michelin recommended restaurants, I preferred eating at a restaurant like this one". I agree and really enjoyed eating at local trattorias.

As noted above, the staff of the dispensary at NAS Sigonella consisted of 12-14 Corpsman, two doctors and two nurses, a dentist and one Dental technician. I have included a pictures of the dispensary group participating in military marching. Although not very athletic I took part in the dispensary baseball teams and had a lot of fun.

Chapter 12

Many military families living on base had dogs as pets and, of course, most took the pets with them when they transferred. One family, for whatever reason, could not take their pet when they transferred and they gave him to another military family on the base. He was a cute little mutt they had named Poncho who did not want to be adopted by another family and kept looking for his original family. When he couldn't find them, he preferred to be free to roam the base and eat at the dining facility with the cooks, who unofficially adopted him. Since a base regulation did not allow stray dogs inside the base and several attempts to capture Poncho failed, being he was a wise little guy, he eluded the Military Police (MP) forcing them to issue an order to shoot him. One night I was with the MPs as they tracked Poncho and I was impressed with his skills in eluding capture and the way he looked. We never had a pet and felt this was a good time to adopt a stray, like Poncho. However, he only trusted the cooks so I talked to them and let them know that if he was not captured he would be killed and asked them to get him and hold him for me, which they did. That day I went and picked him up and took him home. My girls were delighted to have such a beautiful little dog. However, Poncho was not very happy to lose his freedom and just sat in the corner and refused to eat. The next day, as I was going out the door to go to work, Poncho ran out and never looked back. Of course the girls were upset and disappointed but there was nothing I could do. A few days later I spotted him back on the base, he somehow found his way back and joined his friends, the cooks. I again asked the cooks to help me get him back. They were able to get him and called me to pick him up, which I did and took him home for the second time to the delight of my girls. Things were not any better than the first time as he again refused to eat and just sat in a corner. After 2 days I gave up and opened the door pushed him out since it was obvious to me he did not want to be with us. About an hour later we heard scratching at the door and when I opened the door it was Poncho who had returned on his own terms.

Poncho walked in and went to his dish to eat and drink. The girls were thrilled and he stayed close to them and Pat. Poncho came back on his own terms he was, to say the least, a unique dog. He refused a leash, but walked along side of us as if was leashed. He was a super smart dog and when we visited relatives in San Marino he quickly became familiar where they lived and would visit. His favorite place to visit was my uncle Leo's bar/restaurant where Poncho knew he could get treats so, as soon as we arrived in San Marino, he would, on his own, visit him at his bar. I have attached a picture of my Uncle Leo's bar with his wife Tonina where Poncho visited as soon as we arrived. He also visited with my cousins Medana, Lilli (Uncle Leo's children) and Ginetta who is pictured with me and my sister Rita when we were very young. I also included a picture of my Uncle Leo and his wife Tonina at their bar and one of my cousins Medana, Lilli and Ginetta.

When in San Marino we stayed with my aunt (zia) Norina who had never had a pet in her house and initially was reluctant to let Poncho in the house. However, after a couple of days he won her heart and could stay in the house and she even provided a nice blanket for him to sleep on. I have included a picture of Norina at the hospital where she worked. She was a top notch nurse.

All of our other relatives and friends also just loved Poncho and we felt very lucky to have such a smart, beautiful little dog.

As I was coming to the end of my enlistment I had to make a decision to either stay on active duty or accept a discharge. I had almost 10 years of active duty, was an E-6 and had passed the test for promotion to US Navy Chief or E-7 and I liked the Navy, especially being an X-Ray Technician so it made sense I stay on active duty. However, my family and I really enjoyed Italy and wanted to remain, if possible. I contacted my detailer in Washington, DC and told him I would re-enlist if I could get orders to the US Naval Hospital in Naples where they needed an X-Ray Technician, my specialty. In fact, I had been sent to Naples several times to provide X-Ray support. I was surprised and disappointed when the detailer told me he would send me where he decided and not take in consideration any of my preferences. I told him, if that was the case I would get out of the Navy. I'm sure he was certain I would not get out after 10 years on active duty, halfway to retirement and suggested I reenlist and accept whatever orders I would receive. I decided to get out of the Navy and received another Honorable Discharge and left active duty. I made this decision since prior to the end of my enlistment, I had been offered a temporary civil service job in the Supply Department so I had a backup plan. On the day of my discharge I accepted the civil service position and began working as a civilian in the Supply Department at NAS Sigonella.

Chapter 13

Soon after I became a civilian at Sigonella my wife got pregnant and, like the last time, she had to go to the Naval Hospital in Naples one month before delivery. Also, like the last time, I was alone with a full time job and two young daughters. Fortunately, the girls were a little older and could mostly care for themselves and did not have duty nights like when I was on active duty. And more importantly, Donna Marta and the Schillagi family again stepped in to assist me with cooking and taking care of the house and the girls, a true blessing. Carmelo and Filomena also frequently had us over their house for meals. With all the support I had, it was not a difficult time. A month after going to Naples, Pat and I became the proud parents to a beautiful baby girl we named Christina Elizabeth.

Of course our other two daughters were delighted with the new baby sister. We asked Carmelo and Filomena to be proxy God parents and they were happy to do it. We had the baptism in the same main church in Motta and it was a nice ceremony, followed by a small reception at our home. We very happy with this addition to our house as were our friends in Motta. Soon after Christina was born my parents came to for a visit and to meet her. Here is a picture of my mom with Christina on a visit to Taormina and another picture of Christina with our next door neighbors in Motta, a lovely lady and a gentleman, and my grandfather Cristofero.

It was great having my parents visit and we all enjoyed their visit. Soon after their arrival we took them to San Marino and had a great visit with all of our relatives who were happy to see my parents and thrilled to meet Christina. Our American friends on the base were also very happy for us, especially the Atkinson and Haynsworth families. Of course, as you will read below and I discuss, later, Toby Haynsworth was my great boss. Other good American friends were Bob Atkinson a US Navy CDR and a dentist at the base dispensary. His wife, BJ and daughters loved holding Christina and they often visited. One who was not thrilled with the new baby was Poncho, who was initially a little jealous. However, he soon became Christina's guard dog and would not let anyone approach her when she was in her stroller unless we said it was OK with us. Christina was a happy child who loved living in Sicily and grew up speaking both English and Italian to the point where, as young as she was, she often translated for Americans living in Motta. She had a happy childhood with many friends both Italian and American. One of her best friends was Tina, the daughter of a good family friend. Here is a picture of Christina when she was a little older with her guard dog Poncho, who really loved her and she loved him. And a picture of her good friend Tina, who spent a lot of time with Christina at our house.

Christina met some very interesting people. When she was very young she met and was blessed by Cardinal Terence Cook, former Archbishop of New York. Cardinal Cooke, born, raised and ordained in New York City, was consecrated bishop in 1965. From his position of vicar general of the Archdiocese of New York, at the age of 47, he was chosen to succeed Francis Cardinal Spellman as archbishop upon his death in 1967. He also became Military Vicar for the United States and that was the reason he was visiting our military base in Sicily. Cardinal Cooke's cause for sainthood has advanced with the delivery of the relevant documents to the Holy See. Investigations into the life of the much loved Cardinal have begun the "Roman phase" of his path to canonization. Cardinal Cook was kind enough to give my Christina his blessing. When she was at the Rome airport on her way to college she also met and was hugged by Saint Mother Theresa.

Prior to my discharge from the US Navy, because of my language skills and familiarity with the area, I was offered a civilian position in the Supply Department, which I accepted. The position I was offered and accepted was a very low ranking, Clerk Typist, temporary appointment (GS-3). However, given the reasonable cost of living in Sicily at the time, the pay was more than sufficient to maintain a decent standard of living. My wife and girls were delighted that we would remain in Sicily as were all of our Sicilian friends. The same day I was discharged I began working as a clerk typist in the Supply transportation branch. I enjoyed my new job and working with the Italian employees and the US military in the Supply Department. I dealt with military personnel and their families and assisted them in interpreting and settling down in Sicily. In addition to enjoying my job, we also enjoyed doing our shopping in some of the many outdoor markets in Motta and Catania offering a great variety of in season vegetables and fruit.

Chapter 14

A few months after I became a civilian a US Navy Commander, by the name of Hugh (Toby) Haynsworth took over the Supply Department.

I did not realize it at the time but that would be for me a major life changing occurrence. Toby was a red headed friendly looking man with a big cigar in his mouth. I was surprised when he summed me to his office when I thought he didn't even know who I was since I was just a lowly GS-3 employee and he was a US Navy Commander. He began our discussion by reading me the riot act. He wondered why I gave up a very promising US

Navy career and nearly 10 years in the military for a temporary, low ranking civilian position. He pointed out that I was hired as an overseas temporary employee with no job security whatsoever and could be terminated without cause at any time. He wondered what I would do, stranded in Sicily without a job, with a wife and two young children. I am grateful that he was concerned for me and my family and he wanted to assist me in getting my situation stabilized. He arranged for me get some training by sending me to Ft Lee, Virginia to take a very interesting and informative Logistics Management course. He also arranged for me to go to Washington, DC to take a Civil Service exam in order to obtain a career status, which I did on my way back to Sicily. On my return to Sicily, thanks to Toby, I was now a career civil servant and was promoted and put in charge of the Personal Property Office. I also gained an overseas tax free housing allowance that covered my rent.

Soon after I returned and took over the Personal Property Office, all of the Italian employees went on strike and stayed out for over 30 days. Since the office was mostly staffed by Italian employees the strike really impacted on the operation of my office. Nonetheless, service members continued to expect their personal effects be picked up and delivered on time. Since the office had to continue to operate as normal as possible, being in charge, I worked many long hours and weekends to ensure we continued to provide required services with minimum disruption. When the Italian employees walked off the job I was authorized to recruit and hire military family members in addition to some military members. Fortunately I was able to find and hire some very talented and capable family members who required minimum training to assume their duties and did an outstanding job allowing the office to continue operating and to provide required support to military members. Of course, as noted above, I had to put in many hours of overtime to cover for the striking employees. On their return, after more than 30 days, the Italian employees were surprised we were able to continue operating during their strike with minimum disruption. The Personal Property Office was part of the NSA Sigonella Supply Department. Included is a picture taken in 1970 of the Property Office staff.

Soon after the strike was over, operations returned to normal and most of the temporary family member employees were released. I was grateful for their service, they saved the day. One position, would continue to be filled by a family member and was made permanent to ensure continued operations in case of future labor problems.

The only drawback to gaining permanent civil service status was that I was now subject to the civil service rule on overseas assignments, which the assignment was not to exceed 5 years. However, the job security and additional pay was worth the possibility of a transfer. Toby then encouraged (pushed) me to take night college courses, something I had not considered, after all, I had dropped out of high school. With his encouragement and support I enrolled in the University of Maryland, Sigonella campus and took an Italian course, which I enjoyed and easily passed. Toby called me to his office and insisted and pushed me to enroll in other more diverse and challenging college courses. With his encouragement I took a second course, Sociology One with a unique and very good and interesting (hippie looking) instructor and I really enjoyed the course and learned a lot of interesting things and even got an A grade. That pleasant experience prompted me to continue taking courses at Sigonella where in a little more than three years I received a University of Maryland Associate (AA) degree. On my return to the states I enrolled at the University of Maryland Pentagon campus and graduated with a Bachelor Degree in Business Management while working at HQ Military Traffic Management Command (MTMC) in Washington, DC – not bad, in my opinion, for an immigrant high school dropout. I remain very proud of this accomplishment at age 38. My immediate family, including my very proud mother and a niece, came to Washington DC to celebrate with me. Also, a retired US Navy, Chief Gage, who worked for me at Sigonella, came to celebrate. It was a great time.

Toby could not make it but let me know how proud he was of me and I thanked him for his faith in me, he was a great person. If you had the opportunity to read my first book of my life story I talk about Toby who was my boss, mentor and just a good, great and sincere friend. After both Toby and I left Sicily, I went to work at MTMC in Washington, DC and Toby, who in the meantime had retired from the US Navy, was a professor at Winthrop University in Rock Hill, SC. We remained in touch with almost daily email contact, usually discussing politics until his untimely death a few years ago which really saddened me. While at Winthrop Toby co-authored two books with J. Edward Lee: White Christmas in April and given his experience in Vietnam, in 1975 he wrote about the Collapse of South Vietnam where he had served, and the Nixon and the Ford Administrations abandonment of that country. He was also subsequently interviewed on public radio broadcast and featured in The Soldier's Story by Ron Steinman.

Prior to coming to Sigonella, Toby had also been stationed in Madrid, Spain where he became a fan of the great Real Madrid soccer team. He asked me if Catania had a professional soccer team, I told him they did but nothing compared to Real Madrid. He then asked me to take him to the next Catania home game which I did. It was an enjoyable time and he, like me, became a Catania "tifoso" fan. As we continued to attend the home games more and more Americans joined us at the "Cibali" Catania's soccer stadium, including his assistant, LCDR Ed Hernandez. Toby put together a big red and blue flag (Catania team colors) with "Forza Catania Sigonella e con te" (Go Catania, Sigonella is with you) written on the flag. When we hung it up in front of us in the stadium it was a big hit with the local fans as well as the team. The Catania newspaper "La Sicilia" wrote a very nice article on the Sigonella American fans and included a picture of the flag with the article.

At Toby's suggestion, I contacted the team and Toby invited them to visit the Sigonella American base as his guest and they accepted. He sent a bus to pick them up and we took them to the base Officer's club where they enjoyed the American snacks, beer and other drinks. Included is a picture of us at the stadium and some of the players with my friend and Toby's assistant, LCDR Ed Hernandez.

They had a great time and from that day on we could visit the dressing room at the stadium and get together with the players at my home or theirs, it was a lot of fun. Toby, Ed and I, in addition to going to all home games also went to a few Catania games on the road in Naples, Rome other cities in Italy. It was a lot of fun, especially the train rides where we had meals and drank wine with the Italian passengers. On one trip, returning home from Rome, we ran out of wine and when the train stopped in Naples Toby asked (told) me to go buy some wine, which I did. As I was returning with the wine the train started moving and Toby leaned out the train window and instructed me to hand him the wine through the window. I had some difficulty but was able to get on board the moving train a few cars back. When I returned to my seat, out of breath, Toby said it was important he get the wine to him and he was sure I could make it and he wasn't worried – like I was. As noted above, I became a good friend of the entire team and they allowed me to be included in a team picture.

CATANIA 1972-73
IN PIEDI: Guasti, Rado, il tifoso Olimpio, Turchetto, Lodrini, Caruso, Rotolo, Picat Re, D'Amato
SEDUTI: Valsecchi, Gavazzi, Di Bella, Vegni, Fogli, Francesconi, Volpato, Spanio, Simonini
PER TERRA: Colombo, Muraro, Montanari, Ligabue, Puglisi, Scarpa, Giustolisi
ASSENTI: Bernardis, Ghedin, Lausdei, Ventura, Schifilliti.

After Toby left, a group of us, including Ed Hernandez, kept going to the games with a new flag Forza Catania, Sigonella fans. To this day I remain friends with several former Catania players, with one in particular, a former goalie, Luigi (Gigi) Muraro.

Chapter 15

Gigi is from Dueville, a small town in the providence of Vicenza. When he was traded to Catania it was his first time he had been on the island of Sicily. Soon after his arrival we became close friends and he often visited us and soon thereafter he was married in Dueville to a great lady, Ampelia who soon joined him in Catania.

After living in Motta Sant Anastasia for about 10 years our landlord needed the apartment and we had to move. Since we had to move, we decided to get an apartment in the city of Catania and moved to a secure compound. Soon after we moved there several soccer players, including my friend Gigi Muraro and family rented apartments in the same compound. His son Mirko – this is a picture of Mirko and one of my daughters, Christina - was born there soon after they moved in and rented an apartment in the complex. As soon as he could walk, Mirko was a frequent visitor, on his own, to our apartment and spent a lot of time with us, especially with Christina.

My near death experience. A few days before my 30th birthday in 1971, I became ill and in a few days was really sick to the point that I was air evacuated to the US Navy Hospital in Naples. After arriving at the Naples airport I had an interesting ambulance ride through the hectic Naples traffic. When the ambulance arrived at the hospital I was unconscious and immediately placed in intensive care. A series of tests could not determine the cause of my illness and the antibiotics that were initially administered did not have any effect. My illness was a mystery and in a couple of days I became so ill that I was given last rites and my family was asked to come to Naples just in case I did not make it. My wife and three daughters, one only 8 month old, came to visit me but I was unconscious and do not remember their visit or receiving the last rights of the Catholic Church. After trying a variety of antibiotics, on the third day one worked and my condition, although still critical, improved. After a week I began to improve and regained conciseness and was taken off life support and the critical list. After a month in the hospital in Naples I was discharged and taken back to Sicily to continue my recovery at home. Thanks to the good care I received at the Naval Hospital in Naples and then from my wife at home, I was able to return to work after two months. It was a rough time but I am grateful for the care I received at the US Navy hospital in Naples. While I was sick and after I recovered they could not figure out what caused my serious illness but a few years later it was assumed it was Legionnaire disease which was only identified a few years after I was sick.

Fans from the base continued to attend home games and Ed and I and his son occasionally going at away game as far north as Genova. We remained friends with several players. These are my pictures with Romano Fogli and Rino Rado, who was a very good goalie for Catania and the other one with Giorgio Bernardis, a good utility player and another dear friend.

Romano Fogli was a star player who started playing on the Bologna team and then Milan before coming to Catania. He also played several games on the Italian national team. He was an outstanding player, great person and a good friend. Sadly, Romano passed away in 2021, I lost another good friend.

It was a lot of fun being such good friends with the team and even with the team owner, Angelo Massimino. Angelo was a self-made man who made a lot of money in the construction business. He used his money to purchase the team and insisted on managing the day to day operation. He travelled with the team for away games and dined with them as well. For some reason, he took a liking to me and allowed me to also travel, mostly at his expense, with the team and spent time and dined with the players. This was unusual since fans were usually not allowed to frequent players when preparing for a game. Angelo just wanted the Catania team to be as good as possible, spent a lot of money to buy the services of good players and was much appreciated by the fans. During his tenure the team was promoted to series A (the highest Italian professional league) and the fans really appreciated having a team in the top Italian league. The year when the team was in contention to be promoted they won an important game in Reggio, Calabria which assured them the promotion. I was at the game with Massimino and thousands of other Catania fans and, following the win, there were bumper to bumper cars from Messina, across the straights from Reggio all the way to Catania. A normal of less than 2 hour ride took more 8 hours to complete celebrating all the way. It was a lot of fun. Angelo was a very down to earth very simple individual who was not just the owner, but the biggest Catania fan.

Chapter 16

A s I said above, the one player and family we were closest to was Luigi (Gigi) Muraro and his wife Ampelia (Lea). We were also good friends with their families from Dueville, Vicenza. After Gigi and Lea were married they moved in next door to us in Catania and we remained neighbors until I returned to the US. We remain close friends to this day. When I returned to Italy and later was transferred to Vicenza we moved upstairs from them in an apartment they owned. The Murano's are the God parents of my grandson Lorenzo, as can be seen in this photo of the baptism.

I was also good friends with most of the other players and spent a lot of time with them. Included is a picture of Gigi Muraro, Dante Lodrini and Pietro Ghedin with my girls the Ed Hernandez kids and other children.

Thanks to Toby, I gained job security and did not have to worry about losing my job. I had also been promoted to a GS-09 and doing well with my career. However, as noted above, I was now subject to return to the US to a similar position five years after I became a permanent Civil Servant. We decided to cross that bridge when it came and in the meantime we settled down with three children in new residence in the city of Catania. Even after Toby left, a group of Americans from Sigonella led by me and LCDR Hernandez, CDR Stone and others attended all home games and hung a new banner at the stadium. A picture with our new flag since Toby took his with him.

Ed and I and his son also made several trips to other Italian cities to watch our team play and we had a lot fun. After four years my family and I began to be concerned with having to leave Sicily. The two oldest girls were attending Italian school where they felt at home. My wife and I also enjoyed living in Sicily and spending time with the many Italian friends and visiting my relatives in San Marino. I asked for an extension and was told it was not possible and would have to register for placement in a similar position in the United States and would have to accept the first position that was offered or be terminated. I was discussing my dilemma with a good friend and another Catania soccer fan, CDR Art Krzeminski who, at the time happened to be the military dentist at Sigonella and had put braces on my daughter Eva. He suggested I write to the Civil Service Commission and request a two year extension to complete my daughter's dental procedure and he would certify the need for the additional time, which he did. It worked and I was granted a two year compassionate extension for medical reasons. My daughters were delighted but I told them I would register them at the American school on the base so that they would have less difficulties when we returned to the US which we would have to do eventually. They were not thrilled since they liked the

Italian school where they had a lot of friends but realized it would be best for them. Life continued to be good for us and we really enjoyed living in Sicily and having so many Sicilian friends. The two older daughters adapted well to the American school and I was enjoying my job and working with the Italian employees. Pat had many Italian friends in Motta and spent lots of time with a group of women and a seamstress learning the basic seamstress skills and really enjoyed it. We really enjoyed Sicilian food and their desserts. One of the best desserts offered in Sicily are the Sicilian cannoli which we enjoyed with the morning cappuccino or following a good meal.

The cannoli originated in the capital of the Sicilian region, Palermo. Cannoli are pastries consisting of a tube-shaped shells of fried pastry dough and range in size from 9 to 20 centimeters is believed that the cannoli's filling originated with the Saracens, an ancient Arabic peoples, when they brought sugar cane to the region. Cannoli were referred to by the Sicilians as Capelli dei Turchi (Turkish hair), How do Italians eat cannoli? Just like pizza, there are those who pick up cannoli and eat them with their hands and others who prefer to set them on a plate, cutting into pieces with a knife and use a fork to eat a piece at the time. I prefer using my hands and eating them whole. How many flavors of cannoli are there? There are up to 18 cannoli flavors ranging from Hazelnut to Mint chip. The shell is made of honey and almonds, and is crunchy and sweet. Sicilians sell cannoli all year around but most only eat them between autumn and spring and not in the summer. A chocolate chip cannoli is about 400 calories.

One of our best American friends on the base was Ray Larabee who at the time was a Naval Criminal Investigator and we shared an office in at the Sigonella Air base in Sicily. He and his wife Kathy were great friends with our family and their kids were good friends with our children. It was great spending time with them and occasionally taking trips together around Sicily. We met up again a few years later when we were both stationed in Naples. It was really great to meet up with them again. I have included a picture of Ray and his great wife Kathy.

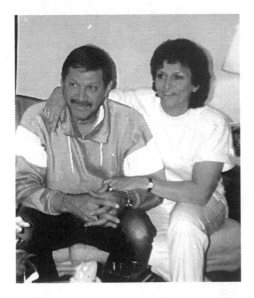

The family and I loved Sicily and the wonderful Sicilians, especially the farmers who still ride donkeys to go to work the land. As discussed above, we lived in the small and wonderful Sicilian town of Motta Sant Anastasia in the providence of Catania for over 10 years and really enjoyed it. We made lifelong friends and our two oldest daughters, attended the local school from pre-school, then 3 and 4 years old, to the eighth grade. They did well with the Italian language while maintaining their English language skills. We then enrolled them in the American school on the military base. I was very happy that they had no problem switching from and Italian school and Italian language to a US school and English. I was and still am very proud of my girls. In addition the Schillagi family, who were more family, than friends, we had many friends in this great little farm town where the shepherds, like my friend, in the picture walked their flock down the main street of the town. Included is a picture of the Shepard and my 1963 VW Bug.

We spent a lot of time with the Schillagi family, which we enjoyed as a family. We also often visited farms around Catania and even had a picnic near Taormina where some of the Godfather scenes were filmed.

I enjoyed, and still enjoy my morning Cappuccino that is the delicious Italian version of coffee, except (in my opinion) a lot better than American coffee. Cappuccino is consumed in the morning at home, like I do now, or like most Italians, including me when I lived in Italy in the morning when I stopped by the local coffee bar for a cappuccino with a variety of delicious pastry, usually consumed standing up at the counter or seated in the bar or at a sidewalk cafe. I really miss that routine in Italy, a country that is known for outstanding food followed by a good cup of espresso coffee after meals. No Italian would ever have a cappuccino after a meal, in Italy, cappuccino is consumed only in the morning with a pastry.

As noted above, we lived in this small agricultural town and made many good friends, some remain lifetime friends. We found the people of this town to be honest, hardworking and just good decent people who accepted us as part of the town from the day we became the first American family in the town. We were welcomed and made to feel part of the town and our two oldest girls were enrolled in the local school and they loved it. In the meantime our youngest Christina, who was born in Naples and like the rest of the family, became very close to all of our Italian friends, especially the Schillagi family. Even after we left Sicily we remained very close to the entire family and we visited them often when stationed in Naples and then when I worked at the US Embassy in Rome where I was responsible to provide NAF Sigonella embassy support so I often visited the area. I have included is a picture of Christina at the wedding of Pino Schillagi and Antonella in Motta on 5 Sept 1981.

Chapter 17

As discussed above, one of my best friends in Sicily was also my boss, a US Navy Commander Toby (Hugh) Haynsworth. Toby was an exceptional and outstanding individual who had made many interesting contacts in his life. One of the most interesting, who Toby introduced me to, was Eugene Mc Donald Bonner, who like Toby, was a native North Carolinian. He was an author, composer, music critic and wayfarer. I met Eugene in Sicily when Toby brought him to the Sigonella Naval base and Toby introduced me to him at the base Officers Club when he was there as his dinner guest. Bonner was a very interesting and unique individual and I really enjoyed meeting and talking to him. For many years Bonner contributed articles on travel, books, drama and music to various magazines and newspapers, both in the United States and Europe.

He frequently visited Sicily beginning right after WW1 and then moved permanently to Taormina in 1956, his and my favorite city in Sicily. Biographical notes for Eugene Mc Donald Bonner: He was born on July 24 Jul 1889 in Jacksonville, North Carolina and lived with his Great Aunt, Mary MacDonald, in Washington, North Carolina from birth to 1907. He then attended the Peabody Conservatory of Music in Baltimore, Maryland from 1907 to1911. From 1911 to 1917 he lived and worked in Europe, primarily in London. He proudly served in the US Army Artillery from1917 to 1919. He then lived and worked in Europe, primarily Paris and London from 1920 to1927. Later he lived and worked, primarily in New York, from1927 to 1955. Then, as noted above, He permanently moved to live and work in Taormina, Italy from 1956 until his death on 8 Dec 1983. He is buried in the Taormina cemetery.

His father was William Tripp Bonner and mother Eugenia Higgins Bonner. As a child, although saddened by the premature death of his mother, he continued to show a preponderant aptitude for art with a particular passion for music that led him, in 1910,

to complete his studies at the Baltimore Conservatory of Music.
From 1911 to 1917, traveling around England, France and Italy,
he continued his studies in composition at the "Landon Ronald"
Conservatory in London. It is precisely in this period that an
important English magazine published a collection of music
composed by Bonner in his youth. He then became a music critic
for the "London Telegraph" and "London Music Standard". During
this period he came into contact with famous musical personalities
of the time, including Enrico Caruso, Arturo Toscanini and Sarah
Bernhardt. He did this until the outbreak of the First World War
and the subsequent US entry into the war. Once the US declared
war, he returned to his native North Caroline to enlist in the US
Army Artillery in order to serve his country. During that terrible
conflict he served in both France and Italy, and rose to the rank
of master Sergeant. While he served in the U.S. Army on at least
one occasion he visited Sicily in the course of his duties. Was it a
secret mission? Since he refers to this mission in vague terms in his
book, who knows? He was, however, revolted by the war, and this
revulsion was given expression in his first major work, the opera
"Barbara Fritchie", based upon Clide Fitch's play about the War
Between the States. In both the play and the opera, the legendary
gray haired Barbara is transformed into a nubile Southern Belle who
falls in love with a handsome Yankee Captain named Trumbull.
It is the story of lovers torn apart and destroyed by war. According
to a member of Winthrop University music faculty, the music is
full of tragic melodies not unlike those found in Puccini's "Madam
Butterfly". In his book American Opera and its Composers, author
Edward Hisper says that the French Conductor Clyde Wolff of the
Paris Opera was so pleased by the score of "Barbra Fritchie" that he
considered producing it himself, but decided against it "as having a
story too distinctly American to appeal to a French audience, and
sadly the American opera impresarios of the day were too enamored
of European Composers to give an American's work a try. After the

First World War, Bonner takes numerous trips to Europe and often visited Taormina, that later became his favorite destinations and eventually his permanent residence. During the years, immediately following the First World War, he wrote and published another important literary effort entitled "The Club in the opera", subtitled "The story of the metropolitan opera club", in which he discusses the stories and intrigues that revolve around this notorious club. From 1920 to 1927 Bonner moved back to Europe continuing to compose and be a music critic. He also collaborates with Anatole France to compose an opera based on the French comedy entitled "Celli qui epousa un femme muette". In 1931 one of his most important works, entitled "The Venetian Glass Nephew", debut on Broadway. This work, set in the eighteenth century, of a satirical and fantastic genre towards the Venetian bourgeoisie, draws inspiration from the ambiguous novel by Elinor Wylie published only five years earlier. The Second World War marks for Bonner a long period of rest from the scene and only later a number of his chamber compositions will be performed by famous musical groups, including the New York Philharmonic, the New York "John Barbirolli" Symphony Orchestra and the Philadelphia Symphony. Between World Wars, Bonner not only composed several operas and other works, but he served as music editor for Outlook magazine and wrote music criticism for a number of different newspapers including the New York Herald Tribune and the London Daily Telegraph. Included is a picture of Bonner as a young composer and another one of Bonner after he settled in Sicily.

After the Second World War, Bonner again visited Europe and often traveled all over Sicily and wrote the book as a first person account of his experience. The book, Sicilian Roundabout, is a remarkable book. While it serves as an excellent guide to all of the most important works of antiquity and places of historical interest on the island, it is really much more. It is a personal memoir of a world traveler, a musician, soldier, and author. Eugene observed that

"Sicily, this irregular triangle of land, set like a jewel in Homer's wine-dark sea and known to the ancients as Trinarcria, has since come to be regarded by not a few poets and scalars as the mythical Garden of Hesperides". Eugene wrote and updated his book based on his personal experience. Eugene was a great story teller, and in this manner of a man telling a favorite tale to his friends that Sicilian Roundabout is written. It is with this friendly tone that the history of numerous waves of immigrants and even invaders is told to his audience. The facts are all there, but they are presented in the context of leisurely trips back and forth across the island. The people joining Bonner on these trips are personalities that add to the fun of it. It isn't just sightseeing, it's a series of entertainments shared with the reader. Because Sicilian Roundabout is so beautifully written, and since the historical and archeologist facts have really not changed, there is no need to alter Bonner's prose in any way. It is believed, however, to be useful to today's reader to provide a little information about the changes that have occurred in Sicily since 1952 when the first edition was published and updated in 1961. I would have loved to visit Sicily on one of Bonners trips. I recommend, if possible, getting a copy of this great book.

I'll discuss later Bonner's travels and contrast them with what Toby and I found in 1995 when we took a one week trip around Sicily and share what we experienced. Toby and I discussed Bonners' book many times and over many years planned to take a trip to Sicily and retrace, to the maximum extent possible, Bonners adventure around the island. We, finally did it in 1995 a trip that we had planned for many years. First of all, what Toby and I found in 1995 was that there were more people, more traffic, and more restorative work to the old archeological sites than Bonner had experienced. Even many more than I had experienced in my 12 years living and working in Sicily from 1963 to 1976. On our trip in 1995 there were many more busses, trains, and more hotels and restaurants than in Bonners time. And, while things cost more in 1995 than they did in the 1950's and 1960's, especially such labor intensive services as chauffeur driven cars, the island is still a tourist's bargain when compared to the rest of Europe and even northern Italy. It was no surprise that we found the Sicilian people friendly and helpful as they were when Bonner first visited Messina in 1913 and on his later visits as they were for my family and me when we lived there. Also, the beauty of the highly varied landscapes has not diminished one bit. Compared to northern Europe, or even northern Italy, Sicily is found on relatively few tourist itineraries. That may be because it seems to be somewhat out of the way, but it really is much more accessible than it was in Bonner's day. Frequent flights to Palermo and Catania from the major northern cities are available daily and the overnight train trip from/to Milan, Bologna, Rome or Naples is a pleasant one. I took these trips many times and always enjoyed them. There is even the possibility of an overnight ferry boat trip, where one can board the ferry in Naples even with their automobile, if they want, for a trip to the Aeolian Islands, a series of islands north of the main island of Sicily and also to Milazzo in northern part of Sicily. We took this overnight trip on the ferry a few times. Then there are high speed autostradas (expressways) built since World War two that, not only cover the entire length of the Italian boot but, since the late 60's, much of the island itself making travel by automobile fast and comfortable. This last mode also frees one to tour the island not constrained by the schedules of the pre-set itineraries of a packaged tours.

Once he became a permanent resident of Sicily, Bonner noted the island had undergone considerable changes (modernized) since his first visits, although some areas, mostly in the center of the island like Enna, had undergone very few changes. Eugene Bonner's book serves as an excellent guide to all of the most important works of antiquity and places of historical interest on the island. As noted above, Eugene Bonner often traveled all over the island especially after he moved to Taormina. Eugene was a great story teller and in this manner of a man telling a favorite tale to his friends. It is with this friendly tone that the history of numerous waves of immigrants and even invaders is told to his audience. The facts are all there, but they are presented in the context of leisurely trips back and forth across the island. Eugene Bonner's book serves as an excellent guide to all of the most important works of antiquity and places of historical interest on the island. Toby and I believed that the book to be useful to today's reader by providing information concerning the changes that have occurred in Sicily since 1952, when the first edition of the book was published, to 1995 when Toby and I did our own roundabout. As noted above, in 1956 Bonner decided to move-bag, baggage, and grand piano to Taormina. He rented a studio apartment from Antonio and Eva Strazzeri, whom he had met and stayed with on earlier visits to Sicily. Once settled in his new Sicilian residence, Bonner became a well-known, popular member of the Anglo-American artist community of Taormina. In Taormina he continued to write and compose, and also played the organ every Sunday at the small Saint George's Anglican Church. It was in this environment that he composed his last major work; an opera entitled "The Masque of Susannah." Sadly, the score was somehow misplaced when Bonner sent it to New York for performance consideration. He is said to have sent it to "a conductor" in New York and was apparently lost. Amazingly, a microfilm copy was found by Bonners old friend, Alan Hartman who then forwarded the microfilm to the library at Winthrop University in Rock Hill, South Carolina. My friend and former boss, Toby Haynsworth, then a professor at Winthrop told me that plans were made for a production of all or part of this work to be presented there.

Not too many years after Eugene moved into the Casa Strazzeri, a tragedy befell the household that must have brought back memories of the early death of his own mother. Antonio and Eva's daughter and her husband had been blessed with a handsome infant son, but very soon after his birth the father was killed in an accident. Then sadly, shortly thereafter, the mother died of a cerebral hemorrhage, leaving the baby orphaned, and in the care of his loving grandparents. By this time Bonner had really become a member of the Strazzeri family, and the double calamity hit him hard. He grieved along with Antonio and Eva, the grandparents but then decided to assume paternalistic role in helping to raise this boy into a man. Turi (Sicilian for Salvatore), as the baby was named, became Bonner's special music student and protégé. A picture of Bonner with a very young Turi, then Bonner giving lessons to Turi as he got older. Also a picture of Turi as an adult playing the piano on Sunday at Saint George's Anglican Church the only Anglican Church (La Chiesa Anglicana di San Giorgio) in central and southern Italy and Sicily where all services are held in English.

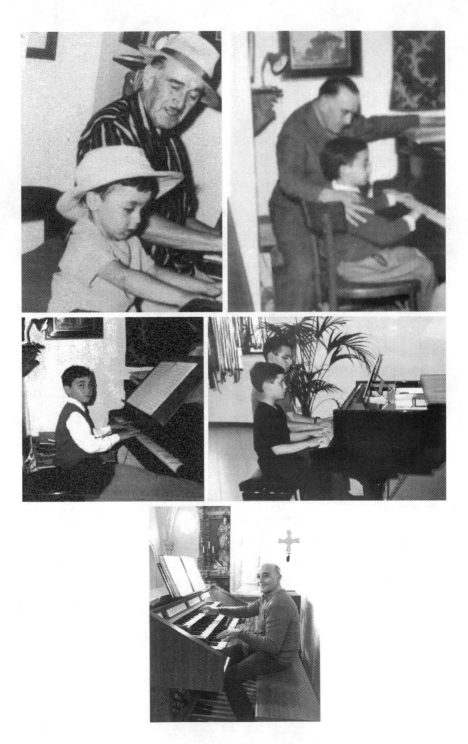

This church was built in the early 1920s by a small group of English people who spent most of the year in Taormina. Taormina's principle Catholic Church is the Chiesa di San Giuseppe, a beautiful church that is dedicated to St. Joseph and located next to the Taormina Clock Tower and faces out onto Piazza IX Aprile. Turi is busy most Sundays playing at both churches like he did when Bonner was alive.

Bonner taught Turi to play the piano and the organ, and he encouraged his natural enjoyment of music. Thanks to Bonner, Turi developed his musical skills and became a professional musician himself. Later, when Turi was older and Bonner found it more difficult to play the church's small pump-organ himself, Turi added the duties of the organist at the Anglicans Church to those he already had at his own principle Taormina Catholic church. The orphaned boy and his surrogate father shared a great love that can still be seen in the eyes of Salvatore LoGiudice, the now grown man himself a father. His younger brother Ivan, who came to know Bonner from his famiy discussions and from reading his music scores. The tradition continues with the second child, Ivan studied music and became a talented musician on the piano (pianoforte) and has a degree as a music instructor. In 2013 his choir, "Piccolo Coro città di Taormina" establised a sister relationship with "Simsbury HS Choir and Orchestra in Saimsbury, Conneticut.

By his 94th year, Eugene Bonner had become somewhat feeble, but he was still mentally alert and took great pleasure in watching the newest member of the Strazzeri clan, Turi's son, take his first steps. On the 8th of December, 1983, Bonner did not feel well. He asked to be helped to the bathroom and once there, he splashed on some cologne and fell over dead. As an Italian obituary writer put it, "To a gentleman, it is crucial to attend important meeting looking his best and smelling good." And so the long happy life of North Carolina native Eugene MacDonald Bonner came to an end in his adoptive home, in the place he loved - Sicily. I visited Bonner's grave in Taormina several times when visiting Sicily and noted that the LoGiudice family took loving care of his burial site.

In recent years, thanks to Toby, there had been a revival of interest in Bonner's music. In 1985 the Charlotte Symphony Orchestra performed his tone poem "White Nights" under the direction of Leon Driehuys, and in 1989, thanks to Toby, the Brevard (NC) Music Center celebrated Bonners centennial of his birth with a performance of "Quintet" for piano and strings with Marilyn Neely at the keyboard. In addition, the Rock Hill Chamber Orchestra, directed by David Lowery, included the suit "Taormina" in its spring program. If the popularity of the artist continued to grow, Eugene Bonner will not be the first artist to achieve greater fame in death than he did in life. I visited the LoGiudice family on several occasions over the years and they always spoke of Bonner with fondness, someone they truly loved and I know he loved them. They have his grand piano in their living room and Salvatore and sons frequently play it. I also met Claudio D'Agata, a Sicilian orchestra conductor who knew and worked with Bonner when they both lived in Taormina. I also met Claudio's wife Bridget and discussed with them Bonner's considerable impact and the love for Taormina. Claudio was a fellow musician who at times performed with Eugene. I have included a picture of Claudio and me in his home in Taormina.

On the dust jacket of his book, Sicilian Roundabout author Eugene MacDonald Bonner is described as being "North Carolina born-author, composer, music critic, and wayfarer." Bonner was all of that, and much more. His aptitude for music was fostered by a next door neighbor, Charlotte Brown, who gave the bright eyed, fun loving little boy his first lessons on the piano. A review of Eugene's "Records for Session," i.e. report cards, shows that while all of his professors acknowledged his superior intelligence, some expressed doubts as to his aptitude for performance. For example, Professor of Organ and Harmony, Harold D. Philips commented after his first year, "very slow in getting his pieces up to the mark, but very sure once mastered. Apt to be rough in his pedaling, but shows taste in registration." Then a year later, "a generally very intelligent student with a good deal of artistic feeling, but very little executive gift and quite out of symphony with the older music." Professor Philip's comments in 1910 seem to predict that Bonner's musical future was to be in composition. "(He) has a good all-around musical intelligence and culture, but no natural gift for concert organ playing. Extemporization and improvisation (are), however, usually good." It was during this period that the

London publishing house, Weeks & Co., brought out a collection of songs written by the young North Carolinian. The magazine Musical America commented on three of them ("A Desert Night-Song", "Pierrot Stands in the Garden", and "Sicilian Boat Song") as follows: "Mr. Bonner shows in all three a creative gift that has much promise. He is not yet mature, nor could one expect it to be since the composer is still a young man. With his musical ideas, he does not strive to be unusual, and his harmonic sense is keen. He also joined in the gaiety of this "Belle Epoque" both in London and on the continent. In 1913 he spent a vacation in Sicily as a guest of the poet Robert Garland, the lyricist for two of the songs mentioned above it is yet to be performed. In addition to publishing a number of songs and chamber works, he collaborated with Anatole France to create and opera based upon the Frenchman's comedy "The Man Who Married a Mute" ("Celui Qui Epousa Un Femme Muette"). Unfortunately, before it could be produced, Anatole French died. Then there were lengthy squabbles with his heirs, producers, and the director of the Theatre Champ-Elysees. The net result of all this was that, once again, a major Bonner work failed to be performed. As best as Toby Haynsworth was been able to find out, the only time the public had a chance to judge the music for itself was when the Baltimore Symphony orchestra performed a "Prelude to the Second Scene of Opera 'La Femme Muette'" on Sunday evening, March 20, 1927. As Bonner himself described the work in an article in the New York Times it is "a straight" little comedy which starts off more or less operatically, but which slips into the spoken drama whenever there's anything of importance to be said or discussed." The critics, including such famous names as Brooks Atkinson, Arthur Ruhl, and Gilbert Seldes, all spoke enthusiastically about the high quality of the music, but somewhat despairingly of the overall production. Some of the specific comments were: "Bonner's music has a delicate sweetness, but when undistinguished actors and singers apply their poor talents to period fantasy, the pleasure runs out of it" (Atkinson). The music was "in keeping with its subject and period and genuinely charming" (Ruhl). "Mr. Bonner, the composer, came off very well" (Seldes). "Mr. Bonner writes with competence and ease in terms of waltzes, folk songs and minuets, and can make emotion mount to recitative, sonorous climaxes. He can be gay, sad, triumphant or severe. He can be elegant, light and fleeting, can put the nocturne note into a serenade, and provide a crisp dance for a Watteau interlude" (unsigned, The Christian Science Monitor). Unfortunately, the show did not catch on, and it closed a week later on the 2nd of March, 1931. I would choose the words of social commentator Dorothy Parker as it's epitaph, "the 'little opera' (was) a moon-lit haven from the boop-boop-a-doops and god dams of Broadway, and as I look back and listen on it, "I think many have spoken too soon about my heart's being completely broken over the current theater." Throughout the Depression and World War II, Bonner was unable to get any of his operatic works staged, although a number of his pieces, songs, and orchestral compositions were performed by such famous musicians as John Barbirolli's New York philharmonic-Symphony Orchestra and Eugene Ormandy's Philadelphia Symphony Orchestra. It was during this period that the London publishing house, Weeks & Co., brought out a collection of songs written by the young North Carolinian. The magazine Musical America commented on three of them ("A Desert Night-Song", "Pierrot Stands in the Garden", and "Sicilian Boat Song") as follows: "Mr. Bonner shows in all three a creative gift that has much promise. It is not yet mature, nor could one expect it to be since the composer is still a young man. His musical ideas a definite, he does not strive to be unusual, and his harmonic sense is keen". Eugene Bonner died on December 8 1983 in Taormina, the town he really loved and where he was loved and where he's buried. As he instructed, all the rights of the musical works and images of Eugene Bonner belong to the Salvatore LoGiudice family, including their children. The Eugene MacDonald

Bonner Collection in North Carolina is a good source for the study of the life of Eugene Bonner. It contains some letters by Bonner himself, plus others by his aunt, Mary Virginia Bonner, and his friends Leon Barzin, conductor and music director of the National Orchestral Association and Alan Hartman, a friend who knew him in New York. My boss and great friend Toby Haynsworth, who, Like Bonner is from North Carolina and he, as discussed above, met Bonner in Taormina. Toby had several taped recordings of Bonner's music, a number of photographs and newspaper articles, and several miscellaneous genealogical references to the Bonner Family. I visited the Strazzeri - LoGiudice family on several occasions over the years and they always spoke of Bonner with fondness, someone they truly loved, as part of their family. They have his grand piano in their living room and Salvatore and sons frequently play it. They also care and maintain his grave in Taormina. Sicily is a beautiful region of Italy, and is the largest region, bigger than Piedmont and Sardegna and is also the biggest Italian island. With 5 million inhabitants, it's the 4th most populated region of Italy. Many areas of Sicily are discussed by Eugene in his book. Toby and I also visited most of these areas while living in Sicily and/or on our one week trip of the island in 1995. Sicily was under Spanish rule from 1190 for over five centuries and was freed by Garibaldi and his Red Shirts during the Risorgimento from the tyranny of Spanish Bourbons, the last region to be freed. During World War 2, the island was liberated by the combined English and American forces after some bitter fighting in 1943 between the Germans and the Allied forces for every square foot of the island. The ports were devastated, the railway system smashed, and hundreds of buildings demolished by the terrific bombing and shelling from the overall attack by land, sea and air. Messina was the Germans last stand on the island prior to their retreat which began on August 11 1943 for a six-day evacuation of the island across the Strait of Messina.

Chapter 18

S ome of the areas and cities in Sicily that Bonner visited and
Toby and I also visited most of them:

Catania: My favorite city in Sicily, where I also lived in
the providence of Catania for 12 years, is an ancient port city on
Sicily's east coast, facing the Ionian Sea. It sits at the foot of Mt Etna
an active volcano with trails leading up to the summit. It is, after
Palermo, the second largest city in Sicily and among the ten largest
cities in Italy. The population of the city proper is 312,000 while
the population of the province of Catania is 1,108,000. Catania
was founded in the 8th century BC by Chalcidian Greeks. The
city has weathered multiple geologic catastrophes. It was almost
completely destroyed by a catastrophic earthquake in 1169. A major
eruption and lava flow from Mount Etna nearly swamped the city
in 1669 and it suffered severe devastation from the 1693 earthquake.
However the Central District or "old town" of Catania features
exuberant late-baroque architecture and is a UNESCO World
Heritage Site. During the 14th century, and into the Renaissance
period, Catania was one of Italy's most important cultural, artistic
and political centers. It was the site of Sicily's first university,
Universita' degli Studi di Catania that was founded in 1434 and is
the 13th oldest university in Italy and the 29th oldest in the world.
Catania has been the native or adopted home of some of Italy's
most famous artists and writers, including the composers Vincenzo
Bellini and Giovanni Pacini and the writers Giovanni Verga, Luigi

Capuana, Federico Capuana and Nino Martoglio. Catania today is the industrial, logistical, and commercial center of Sicily. Its airport, Fontanarossa, is the largest in Southern Italy. The city's wide central square, Piazza del Duomo, features the whimsical Elephant fountain statue (Fontanta dell'Elefante) and the richly decorated Catania Cathedral, as discussed below. In the southwest corner of the square, behind the Cathedral, in the tunnel of the walls of Charles V, there is a fish market which is partly outdoors and partly covered. A place where every day under large red and white awnings and on marble counters, the ritual of selling fish and also meat and fruit takes place, has been repeated since ancient times. The cries of the vendors, the stalls steaming with roasted peppers and sea food sold to passers-by make this place one of the most emblematic topic of the city. It's the ideal place to immerse oneself in the local Catanese culture and be fascinated. When we lived in Catania province we often visited the fish market and also ate there and yes, we did immerse ourselves in the Catanese culture – great experience. The Cathedral, which contains the relics of its patron Sant Agata, was originally erected in 1355, to be rebuilt after the tragic earthquake of Val di Noto, in the early 1700s. It has since become a symbol of Catania, recognizable by the arch which opens onto via Crociferi. It connects the great abbey, which includes the Church of San Benedetto, the pearl of Catanese baroque architecture. Also, the Palazzo Biscari, the most important palace in the city. It represents, in fact, the most beautiful example of Catanese baroque architecture. The building, after the earthquake of 1693, was rebuilt around 1700 by Ignazio Paternò Castello III, the fifth Prince of Biscari, and a great scholar, archaeologist and art lover. In addition to making Catania his home, he established the first major museum, containing his large archaeological collection and is open to all. In 1787 the prince received Goethe who then reported in detail in his writings the magnificence of the collections and the palace. History, charm and beauty are the words required to describe the building, a magnificent example of Sicilian masterpieces. The Piazza Duomo (Cathedral square) in the very center of Catania. The splendid Norman Cathedral, dedicated to the Patron Saint of the city, Sant Agata. From the city center of Catania you get a beautiful view of MT Etna. Together with other famous Catanesi, Vincenzo Salvatore Carmelo Francesco Bellini was an Italian opera composer, who was known for his long-flowing melodic lines for which he was named "the Swan of Catania". He is one of the most famous citizens of Catania and is buried in the main and beautiful Cathedral of Catania.

The columns on the lower level in the cathedral belonged to the original ancient structure. The statue of the elephant with his trunk pointed at the cathedral as to pay homage to its Patron Saint is located right in front of the Cathedral. Elephant Palace (Palazzo degli Elefanti), that is now the local municipal building, is also located on the square.

My family and I lived for 12 wonderful years in the province of Catania, 8 years in Motta Sant Anastasia and 4 in the city of Catania itself and we loved it – a beautiful city, with beautiful and caring people we loved. When we lived there, Catania had a decent soccer team as discussed above which I enjoyed, along with other Americans being a fan.

Giardini Naxos: Was a Greek colony and was founded in 734 BC by the Calcidesi d'Eubea coming from a big island located in the Aegean Sea. Hippocrates, tyrant of Gela, captured Naxos in 494 BC. The opposition of Naxos to Siracusa ultimately led to its occupation and destruction in 403 BC at the hands of Dionysius, the tyrant after Naxos supported Athens during that city's disastrous Sicilian Expedition. Today it is part of the providence of Messina and is located on the east coast of the island and sits in front of the Ionian Sea on a bay which lies between Capo Taormina and Capo Schisò. Naxos was never a powerful city, but its temple of Apollo Archegetes, protecting deity of all the Greek colonies, gave it prominence in religious affairs. Leontini and Catania were both colonized by inhabitants of Naxos. Though the site continued to be inhabited, most activity shifted to neighboring Tauromenium (Taormina). In 1544, following the raids by corsair, Kheir-ed-Din, several military buildings were constructed to protect Cape Schisò from the Barbary pirates who continued to attack and plunder the coastal villages. This was Schisò Castle, which was rebuilt from an earlier 13th-century castle and Vignazza Tower. The latter is a four sided watchtower which served to observe the coast south of Port Schisò. It was constructed in 1544 to serve as a watch tower for Cape Schisò and the coast south of Port Schisò against the raids of the Barbary corsairs led by the a Turkish corsair. When an enemy ship was sighted, the guardian of the watchtower could alert the villagers and neighboring watchtowers by sending out smoke signals. Vignazza Tower is located in the Recanati area of Giardini Naxos and is annexed to the archeological park. Its interior is still occasionally used for exhibitions and performances. We enjoyed visiting the beach of Giardini Naxos and relax after a day trip to the beautiful town of Taormina, one of my family's favorite places on the island.

Taormina: And then there is Eugene Bonner's old haut, and his favorite (and mine as well) town in Sicily and his future residence. Taormina happens to be the youngest of all Greek cities in Sicily. It was founded in the year 306 BC. The story of Taormina has its origins in and is interwoven with that of Giardini-Naxos, the first Greek colony in Sicily, founded by Teocle and then destroyed by Dionysius (430–367 BC). The survivors of the destruction moved to Mount Taurus where they founded the beautiful town of Taormina (Tauromenion), perched on a cliff on the east coast of Sicily with a stunning view overlooking the modern day Naxos, the Ionian Sea and a great view of an active volcano, Mt Etna. Taormina has always been an attraction to tourists. Toby and I ran across a travel guide to Sicily written by an Englishman who lamented that Taormina was "being ruined by all the tourist from the north". That was written in the last century, and the complaint can still be heard today. But the place continues to cast a spell that attracted travels even in the days of antiquity. It is a beautiful mediaeval town that my family, like many Americans from Sigonella, often visited. Taormina is best known for the "Teatro Antico di Taormina" an ancient Greco-Roman theater. This architectural marvel is not just a sterile relic of history, but a living playhouse, remains operational and it currently used for dramatic works, both modern and classic and also used for various performances and activities, including a beauty contest.

The Greco-Roman Theater was built originally by the Greeks when the city was one of the richest and most powerful in Sicily. It was reconstructed at a much later period by the Romans. The view of Mt Etna from the main piazza is timeless, the only question is whether or not is more spectacular than that from the Geek Theater. Besides the ancient Greek Theater the town has lovely gardens, alleys to wonder and explore, and a stunning views of an active Volcano and the sea. There are also many old, historic churches and many other tourist attractions. Taormina's main street (the

Corso) is jammed by tourists on Saturday and Sunday afternoons. Be aware that at the height of the season, hotel rooms can be scarce as it remains a favorite tourist destination. Its character has changed little from Gene's time. His favorite café, the Shaker Bar, is still there, filled with folks enjoying their aperitifs in the open air. I enjoyed frequenting the Shaker bar on my visits to Taormina. Taormina is currently considered by many the tourist capital of this beautiful island, although there are many other beautiful and interesting places to visit on the island.

Trouble came to this once beautiful and peaceful place when, in the middle of the twentieth century when World War II arrived. With the military alliance of Fascist Italy and Nazi Germany, Taormina found itself, not too willingly, the Sicilian Headquarters of the German General Staff. In the early summer of 1943, the liberating Anglo-American forces landed on the south coast of Sicily and the entire island became one huge battleground. As the headquarters of the Germans in Sicily, Taormina experienced more than its share of trouble. The Nazis had installed themselves in the celebrated and beautiful Hotel San Domenico which had become the nerve center of their operation. The Americans and English had no choice but to bomb the hotel from the air and sea. As a result, the damage and loss of life were considerable. The San Domenico church adjoining the San Domenico hotel was also, along with the hotel, blown to bits and the lovely old Chiesa Del Carmine was reduced to a gutted ruin. Also destroyed was the medieval gateway known as "Porta Tocco". However, according to Bonner, all things considered the overall damage sustained by the town was surprisingly small. With the exception of the aforementioned damage none of its most famous monuments such as the Greco-Roman Theater and the Badia Vecchia did not sustain any serious damage. The San Domenico hotel was rebuilt and is currently a favorite destination for many tourists.

The Aeolians Islands are one of 55 UNESCO World Heritage sites in Italy. They are located off the northern coast of Sicily, and offer seas as clear as the Bahamas, landscapes worthy enough to be film sets and exceptional restaurants. They are: Vulcano, Lipari, Stromboli, Panarea, Filicudi, Alicudi, and Salina. The seven pearls of Sicily all have the same volcanic origins but they are, at the same time, both so similar and so different in terms of their structure and morphology. My family and I loved visiting and lodging on some of these beautiful islands.

Lipari is the largest and most populated of the Aeolians. The island has the biggest town of the archipelago, also called Lipari. It's a lively busy place with picturesque streets, an attractive harbor and a historic castle-citadel. Like its island neighbors, Lipari has volcanic origins. The last eruption on the island took place around 1,400 years ago. There are currently no signs of volcanic activity other than thermal springs and fumaroles on this island. The island's geology is the most visible reminder of Lipari's origins. Until recently one of its main industries was extraction of pumice, created by past eruptions. The thermal springs offer a warm, relaxing swim which we really enjoyed. The island's population is around 10,000.

Vulcano is, has the name indicates, clearly of volcanic origin. Beautiful beaches and thermal waters and mud will relax you while your skin will be grateful. My family and I often took advantage of relaxing mud baths. The last reported eruption of the volcanoes occurred over a two-year period between 1888 and 1890. Since then, their activity has never completely ceased, but it's not a pressing concern for visitors. The 'fumaroles' springs are the only visible manifestations of volcanic activity after the last considerable eruption occurred in 1890. This entire island seems to exist for the purpose of relaxing visitors with its mud baths, crystal-clear water, and impressive vista views on extensive hiking paths. I agree that Vulcano is a remarkable volcanic island that features clear waters, breathtaking hiking paths, and activities to relax you. On our visits my family and I stayed on this island and enjoyed the beach, thermal springs and the mud baths. It has a permanent population of approximately 1000.

Salina is the greenest and most cultivated of the islands of the Aeolians. With its three towns, Santa Marina, Malta and Leni, it is the second largest of the Aeolian Islands, with a population of little more than 2,300 inhabitants. The green hills that sit high above the sparkling Tyrrhenian Sea are beautiful.

Stromboli with its black sand and whitewashed houses, has been the most famous of all the islands since ancient times on account of its volcanic activity. Mount Stromboli, one of the three active volcanoes in Italy has been in almost continuous eruption for the past 2,000–5,000 years. Its name is derived from the Ancient Greek name *Strongýlē*. The minor eruptions, often visible from many points on the island and from the surrounding sea, giving rise to the island's nickname "Lighthouse of the Mediterranean". The island's population is about 500. We had the experience and pleasure of watching it erupt and see the hot lava flow in the Mediterranean – quite a sight.

Alicudi is the westernmost of the eight islands that make up the Aeolian archipelago. The island is about 40 km west of Lipari, has a total area of 5.2 km^2, and is roughly circular. Today there are around 120 inhabitants who mostly live off fishing, or the small agriculture of the island.

Filicudi is situated about 30–50 km northeast of the island of Sicily. Has area of 3.664 mi^2 and a population of 235.

Panarea is the smallest of the seven inhabited Aeolian Islands, a volcanic island chain in north of Sicily. It is part of the town of the island of Lipari and of the providence of Messina. This chic little island attracts VIPs, celebrities and Italy's wealthy who come in the summer for yachting breaks, romantic escapes and late-night partying on terraces with views. While prices may be high and some of the visitors annoying in the peak season of July and

August, outside this period the island is a peaceful paradise with very reasonable prices. Visit in May, June or September, October and you're likely to find sunshine, beauty, tranquility, sea-views and an air of charmed exclusivity mixed with island simplicity – all within a moderate budget. It has a permanent population of approximately 1300.

Pelagie Islands.

Lampedusa is one of the Pelagie Islands. It's known for its beaches, including the Spiaggia dei Conigli (Rabbit beach), with shallow waters and colorful marine life. It faces the Area Marina Protetta Isole (protected Islands) Pelagie on the south coast, and is a protected egg-laying site for marine turtles. Farther east, the smaller Cala Greca is a sheltered beach. Dolphins inhabit the waters around the island. It covers an area of 7.799 mi^2 with a population of 6,556. I loved visiting there when we had a US Coast Guard base and I provided the base with US Embassy support. I enjoyed very much the beautiful beach and the great local food.

Linosa is another of the Pelagie Islands located in the Sicily Channel and is part of the municipality of Lampedusa and the province of Agrigento.

Lampione is a small rocky island located in the Mediterranean Sea, which is one of the Pelagie Islands and administratively part of the commune of Lampedusa and Linosa, in the Province of Agrigento. The small island is about 200 meters (656 feet) long and 180 meters (591) feet across. It has an area of 4 hectares (9.9 acres) and the highest elevation on the island is 36 meters (118 feet). The island is uninhabited and the only building on the island is an unmanned lighthouse. Lampione is part of the "Riserva Marina Isole Pelagie", and its vegetation and wildlife reserve are strictly protected. Several protected animal species inhabit the island. Numerous migrating birds also inhabit the island. The waters are populated by sharks, including the sandbar shark, groupers, lobsters, and varieties of yellow and pink coral.

Pantelleria, the ancient Cossyra or Cossura is the largest among the minor islands of Sicily. It's the nearest Italian island to Africa, only 70 km, and on clear days Tunisia is visible. It is 100 km southwest of the main island of Sicily. Its spectacular landscapes show the volcanic origins of the island. The population is approximately 7,500.

Ustica is a small island in the Tyrrhenian Sea. It is about 5 kilometers across and is situated 52 kilometers north of Capo Gallo, Sicily. Roughly 1,300 people live in the town by the same name. There is regular ferry service from the island to Palermo.

Messina Ancient Greek city It is the third largest city on the island of Sicily, and the 13th largest city in Italy, with a population of more than 231,000 inhabitants in the city proper and about 650,000 in the Metropolitan City. It is also known for its Norman Cathedral, with its Gothic portal and 15th-century windows. The bell tower houses a beautiful clock, the largest due its location astronomical clock in the world which comes to life every day at noon. My family and I had the pleasure of witnessing this beautiful clock come to life many times.

The Cathedral was built by the Normans and was consecrated in 1197 by Archbishop Berardo. There is also the Fontana di Orione with its carved inscriptions and the Neptune Fountain, topped by a statute of the Sea God. Henry VI, Holy Roman Emperor and Constance I of Sicily, were present to witness the consecration ceremony of the Cathedral. The current building is the result of some major twentieth-century reconstruction which took place following the disastrous earthquake that struck Messina in 1908 when only the perimeter walls, the Gothic portal and an apse remained standing. The catastrophic earthquake also destroyed surrounding buildings in Piazza Duomo and only an original mosaic and statue survived. There was also considerable damage resulting from the heavy aerial bombardment in World War II. In 1943 incendiary bombs fell on the restored roof destroying much of its interior. Messina is located near the northeast corner of Sicily and is Sicily's link to the Italian mainland via frequent ferry boats that carry passengers, automobiles as well as trains between Messina and Villa San Giovanni and Reggio, Calabria on the mainland. For many years the construction of a bridge with the mainland has been discussed but, to date, only some projected drawings have been made. Today Messina remains a thriving port and is hugely important for the economy of Sicily as well as the rest of Italy. The city's main resources are its seaports, tourism, commerce, and agriculture. Wine production and cultivating lemons, oranges, mandarin oranges, and olives. The city has the University of Messina, a state university as founded in 1548 by Pope Paul III, it was the world's first Jesuit College and today it is counted among the oldest universities in all of Italy.

Siracusa, Greatest of all Geek Cities: Siracusa, described by Cicero, over two thousand years ago, as "the greatest of all Greek cities", was the principle Greek city in Sicily. It was also the biggest and one of the most powerful cities in the ancient world. It is located on the Ionian Coast of Sicily and is best known for

its ancient ruins. The Archaeological Park is comprises of both
the "Teatro Greco" and the "Roman Amphitheater" as well
as the "Orecchio di Dionisio", (Dionisio Ear) a limestone cave
shaped like a human ear. The Archeologico Museum, Paolo Orsi,
exhibits terracotta artifacts, Roman portraits, and Old Testament
scenes carved into white marble. The principal Greek Temples
and theaters are crowded into a much smaller area than have been
provided for them at Segesta and Selinunte and are fenced in for
security. The fame of these Siracusan sites attract many tourists,
so expect them to be more crowded especially the small island of
Ortygia (Ortigia). For those who like to visit castles, you are in the
right place. They are Mania and Eurialo Castles that are among
the most picturesque castles on the Island of Sicily. Maniace Castle
is named after the Byzantine Commander Giorgio Maniace. It's a
true symbol of the power and the genius of Emperor Federico II,
who built it upon an ancient fort between 1232 and 1240.

Immersed in the colors of the sea, at the most extreme flap of
land on the Island of Ortigia is Eurialo Castle, one of the largest
and most complete military works of the Greek period. It was built
by Dionysus I, tyrant of Siracusa in order to complete the great
defensive system called Dionysian walls, which ran alongside the
edge of the plateau of Epipoli. Also known as Città Vecchia. The
small island of Ortigia, is the oldest part of the beautiful city of
Siracusa and the city is rightly one of the most popular destinations
in eastern Sicily and the small island of Ortygia is the historical
center of the city. Walking through the ruins is like going back in
time as they still resound with the clatter of the soldiers' sandals.

Temple of Apollo: The magnificence of these Greek ruins can
be immediately noticed when arriving on the island of Ortigia.
It is the oldest Doric temple in Sicily and its story has been very
troubled over time. It was first a Christian church, then a mosque,
then again a Norman church and finally a barracks at the time of
Charles V. In the evening, thanks to the lights of the city, one can

enjoy a unique spectacle. The temple's stylobate (a continuous base supporting a row of columns in classical Greek architecture) is the top step of the "crepidoma". Crepidoma is an architectural term for part of the structure of ancient Greek buildings and is the multilevel platform on which the superstructure of the building is erected. The crepidoma usually has three levels and each level typically decreases in size incrementally going upwards, forming a series of steps along all or some sides of the building. The crepidoma rests on the foundation which historically was constructed of locally available stone. The platform was built on a leveling course that flattened out the ground immediately beneath the temple. The construction of a building with forty-two monolithic columns, probably transported by sea, must have seemed, at the time, incredible to its builders as demonstrated by the unusual inscription on the top step on the eastern face dedicated to Apollo in which the builder (or the architect) celebrates the construction of the building with an emphasis on the pioneering character of the construction. The remains permit the reconstruction of the original appearance of the temple, which belongs to the proto-doric or pertaining to architecture, as in certain Egyptian tombs. The pioneering building was a defining step in the emergence of the Doric temple in Sicily, representing a sort of local prototype. A very interesting area to visit for sure which Toby and I really enjoyed visiting.

Agrigento: In our 1995 tour of Sicily, after a half a day in a crowded Siracusa Toby and I spent much of the afternoon on the road when we traveled from Siracusa to Agrigento by rental car and it took us longer than we anticipated, but it turned out to be a blessing. We spent a quiet evening in a comfortable hotel and had a great Sicilian sea food dinner. It worked out perfectly and it gave us an early start for a visit to the beautiful Valley of the Temples (which is really on a hill top within the valley).

Agrigento is one of the oldest cities in Sicily, founded in 581 B.C. by Greek settlers Rodio-Cretan and became Akragas in the following century. It is a city located on a hilltop on Sicily's southwest shore. It's known for the ruins of the ancient city of Akragas located in the Valley of the Temples, a vast archaeological site with well-preserved Greek temples. It has risen several times on its ancient remains and has represented one of the most shining Centers of the Mediterranean. About 2500 years ago, the tyrant Theron had a system of tunnels and hypogea (the subterranean part of an ancient building also an ancient underground burial chamber) designed to feed this small valley with water. The large swimming pool that emerged became a meeting place for the rich inhabitants of the city. A century later it was buried and gave rise to a very fertile garden comparable to Eden. On the modern city's outskirts is the Museo Archeologico Regionale 'Pietro Griffo', with artifacts and a telamon (giant male figure). On the west of the city lies Scala dei Turchi (Ladder of the Turks), a stepped white cliff overlooking sandy beaches. In 1934, Count Alfonso Gaetani, from Naro, a small village with a beautiful castle rich in medieval monuments, was looking for an idea to promote the typical products of Agrigento, so was born the Almond Blossom Festival. The festival in the early days was an exhibition of floats and island folk groups, but over the years it has evolved to attract the participation from the rest of Italy, Europe and even overseas. From this initiative was born the "International Festival of Folklore" which is celebrated every year between February and March when the almond trees blossom and the valley is filled with a pleasant aroma (I loved visiting in this period). In this period the Valley of the Temples lives a week of celebration and meeting people from many nations. The highlight is the evocative lighting of the tripod of friendship in front of the Temple of Concord.

Enna: Stands at almost 1,000 meters above sea level and is also one of the few big Sicilian cities that is not located the coast, lying inland in almost the exact center of the island. The hilltop setting not only makes it more pleasant in Sicily's often scorching summer heat, but also means that it has views from nearly every terrace, giving it the nickname of Sicily's Belvedere. The Castello di Lombardìa (Lombardy Castle) is an important military structure in Sicily. It was built by Sicanians, rebuilt by Frederick II of Sicily, and restructured under Frederick II of Aragon. The castle is named for the garrison of Lombard troops that defended it in the Norman era. It has an irregular layout which once comprised 20 towers. Of the six remaining towers is the Torre Pisan, which is the best preserved tower. The castle was divided into three different spaces separated by walls. The first courtyard is the site of a renowned outdoor lyric theater, the second one houses a large green park, while the third courtyard includes the vestiges of royal apartments, a bishop's chapel, medieval prisons, and the Pisan Tower.

The Cathedral of Enna was built in the 14th century by queen Eleonora, Frederick III's wife. It was renovated and remodeled after the fire of 1446. The interior has a nave with two aisles, separated by massive Corinthian columns and three apses. The stucco decoration is from the 16th and 17th centuries. Art works include a 15th-century crucifix panel painting, a canvas by Guglielmo Borremans. The cathedral's treasure is housed in the Alessi Museum, and includes precious ornaments, the gold crown with diamonds known as the "Crown of the Virgin," Byzantine icons, thousands of ancient coins, and other collections. The Palazzo Varisano was adapted to house the Regional Archaeological Museum of Enna. It has material dating from the Copper Age to the 6th century AD, recovered from many archaeological areas. Torre di Federico, is an octagonal ancient tower that was thought to be a summer residence of Frederick II of Hohenstaufen. It was part of a bigger complex, named Old castle and destroyed by Arabs. Remnants include some pieces of the old, imposing walls on the top of the green hill where the Tower rises.

Palermo: Is Sicily's capital and largest city, human settlement in the area goes back to prehistoric times and is one of the most ancient sites in Sicily. Interesting graffiti and prehistoric paintings were discovered in the Addaura grottoes in 1953 by archaeologist Jole Bovio Marconi. They portray dancing figures performing a propitiatory rites. Palermo was founded by Phoenician traders in the 8th century BC. Between the 8th and the 7th centuries BC, the Greeks colonized Sicily. They called the city Panormos ("All port"). In the course of the Punic Wars Palermo was fought over by the Carthaginians and the Romans until 254 BC when the Roman fleet besieged the city. Palermo decayed under Roman rule but prospered when the Byzantine general Belisarius recovered it from the Ostrogoth. They imposed a lasting Roman rule over the town known as Panormos, a flourishing and beautiful city during the Golden Age of the Roman Republic and Empire. In 535, the Byzantines stormed the port which soon turned into the fierce and disastrous Gothic War. The Byzantine rule lasted until 831, when the Arabs captured Palermo after a year-long siege and made it the capital city of their Sicilian emirate. The Arab rulers allowed the natives freedom of religion on the condition that they paid a tax. Although their rule was short in time, it was then that Palermo (called *Balharm* in Arabic) displaced Siracusa as the prime city of Sicily. However, the Arab emirate became increasingly torn by inner disputes and was a rather easy prey for the Normans who entered Sicily in 1061 and in 1072 it returned Sicily under Christian rule. However, traces of the ancient Arab domination can still be seen even today. Christianity was restored as the official religion and declared Palermo to be the capital of the island. In 1130, Roger II was crowned the King of Sicily. Not far from the city of Palermo, in the town of Monreale, where there is a beautiful cathedral, "the Cappella Palatina" built by Roger II. It was the second important church erected at the initiative of this king, its construction began in 1132 and completed in 1140. The Cappella Palatina was built by Normans of French descendants.

Although Christians, the Normans were tolerant towards the Muslim population, which at the time was a majority in Palermo and Jews also remained an important community. Sicily in 1194 fell under the control of the Holy Roman Empire and in 1713, Sicily was handed over to the Savoia. From 1820 to 1848 all Sicily was shaken by upheavals, until January 12, 1848. After the Siege of Palermo in again in May 1860, when Giuseppe Garibaldi entered the city with his troops ("I mille - the Thousand"). After the plebiscite, later that year, Palermo and the whole of Sicily became part of the new Kingdom of Italy. From that year onwards, Palermo followed the history of Italy and as the administrative center of Sicily. Today, Palermo, Sicily's biggest city with 720,000 inhabitants but is still struggling to recover from the devastation of the Second World War. In 1943, during World War II, the Allies began to advance up Italy and, following the Allied invasion of Sicily, in July the harbor and the surrounding quarters were heavily bombed by the Allies and the area was all but destroyed. In 1946 the city was declared the seat of the Regional Parliament, and in 1947 became the capital of the Region of Sicily with a special status whose seat is in the Palazzo dei Normanni (Norman Palace). Palermo's future seemed to look bright again but unfortunately, mostly because of the Mafia, it did not happen. Many civil servants lost their life in the struggle against the criminal organizations of Palermo and Sicily. These included the Carabinieri General Carlo Alberto Dalla Chiesa, the region's president Piersanti Mattarella, also, Pino Puglisi, a priest, and magistrates such as Giovanni Falcone and Paolo Borsellino. The latter was killed in July 1992, together with five members of his security detail, in a massive car bombing in Via D'Amelio in Palermo. In spite of many problems, Palermo is nonetheless an important trading and business center and the seat of a university frequented by many students from Islamic countries, as the city's relationship with the Muslim world never ceased. Palermo is connected to the mainland through an international airport and an increasing number of maritime links. However, there is no land connections to the mainland. This fact and other reasons, such as crime, unfortunately have thwarted the development of tourism in this beautiful and historic island. Another factor was the reduced importance of agriculture that led to a massive migration to the cities, especially Palermo, which swelled in size. However, instead of rebuilding the city center the town was thrown into a frantic expansion towards the north, where practically a new town was built, but without parks, schools, public buildings, proper roads and the other amenities that characterize a modern city. The Mafia played a huge role in this process, which was an important element in the Mafia's transition from a mostly rural phenomenon into a modern criminal organization. As noted above, Palermo is Sicily's biggest city and the capital of the Region.

Corleone: Is a town of roughly 11,000 inhabitants with a density of 49 inhabitants per square kilometer and is part of the Metropolitan City of Palermo. The territory of Corleone has been inhabited since prehistoric times. Recent research has identified several settlements distributed around two main areas. In 840 AD, Corleone was conquered by the North African Aghlabids during the Muslim conquest of Sicily. It was during the Muslim occupation that it gained economic, military and strategic importance. In 1080 the city was conquered by the Normans and in 1095 it was annexed to the Diocese of Palermo. Even in the 1170's 80% of the population of the area was Muslim, including those bearing Arabic–Islamic names. Corleone is located in an inland area of a mountain, in the valley between the Rocca di Maschi, the Castello Soprano and the Castello Settimo. Corleone is also the birthplace of several fictional and real characters in Mario Puzo's 1969 novel, the Godfather, including Vito Corleone. The film the Godfather and in the first two of Francis Ford Coppola's film trilogy are based on Corleone. Vito Corleone was originally portrayed by Marlon Brando in the 1972 film and later by Oreste Baldini as a boy and by Robert DeNiro as a young man in The Godfather, Part II. Several Mafia bosses have come from Corleone, including Tommy Gagliano, Gaetano Reina, Jack Dragna, Giuseppe Morello, Michele Navarra, Luciano Leggio, Leoluca Bagarella, Salvatore Riina and Bernardo Provenzano. The Corleonesi led the Mafia in the 1980s and 1990s, and were the most violent and ruthless group ever to take control of the organization.

Marsala: A town in the western part of Sicily. It is situated on Cape Boeo, south of Trapani. It was founded by the Carthusians in 397-398 BC after the destruction of the offshore island of Motya by Dionysius tyrant of Siracusa. Marsala is best known for its wine by the same name. Dry Marsala is typically used for savory entrées where it adds a nutty flavor and caramelization to beef tenderloin, mushrooms, turkey and veal. Sweet Marsala is typically used to make very sweet and viscous sauces. Marsala is also one of my favorite dessert wines to sip. This wine has a unique taste for two reasons: the use of only Sicilian indigenous grapes and a very complex winemaking process. This fortified wine was probably first popularized outside Sicily by the English trader John Woodhouse in 1773, when he first landed at the port of Marsala and discovered the local wine produced in the region, aged in wooden casks and tasted similar to Spanish and Portuguese fortified wines at that time popular in England.

Morgantina: Only a few kilometers down the road towards Catania from Piazza Armerina is the recently discovered the city of Morgantina. While archeologists are still busy uncovering new sections of the site, there is much that can already be seen. It is an archaeological site in east central Sicily, It is sixty kilometers from the coast of the Ionian Sea, in the province of Enna. The closest modern town, two kilometers southwest of the site, is Aidone. The site consists of a two-kilometer long ridge running southwest-northeast, known as Serra Orlando, and a neighboring hill at the northeast called Cittadella. Morgantina was inhabited in several periods. The earliest major settlement was made at Cittadella and lasted from about 1000/900 to about 450 BC. The other major settlement was located on Serra Orlando, and existed from about 450 BC to about 50 BC. Morgantina has been the subject of archaeological investigation since the early 20th century.

Serra Orlando was identified as Morgantina by Kenan Erim, following the discovery of a number of coins bearing the Latin word Hispanorum Erim. These coins were used for passages from Livy. It is believed that the city found at Serra Orlando was in fact the ancient city of Morgantina.

Caltagirone. The city's name derives from the Arabic "qal'at-al-jarar" ("Castle of [pottery] jars") – a name that attests to the antiquity of the pottery works which are still thriving. Caltagirone was inhabited since prehistoric times as evidenced by the presence of two necropolis dating from the second millennium BC and by numerous other archaeological finds. It was later inhabited by the Sicels pre-Roman population. The main landmark of the city is the 142-step Monumental Staircase of Santa Maria del Monte, built starting in 1608 in the old part of the town. The peculiarity is that each step is decorated with different hand-decorated ceramics, using styles and figures derived from the millennial tradition of pottery making. It is a beautiful staircase that we enjoyed visiting many times as a family and with friends. I have included is a picture of the staircase and one with my wife Pat, daughter Christina is our good friend Debbie Burke.

Once a year, on and around 25 July the day of the city's patron saint, St. James, the staircase is illuminated with candles of different colors arranged in order to reconstruct an artistic drawing of several meters. Caltagirone flourished under the Normans and Hohenstaufen, becoming a renowned center for ceramics and the production of other pottery, particularly maiolica, and terra-cotta wares. Nowadays, the production is more and more oriented to artistic production of ceramics and terra-cotta sculptures. Other activities are mainly related to agriculture and tourism. The city was almost completely destroyed in 1693 by a Magnitude 7.4 earthquake that hit the island. Many public and private buildings that were destroyed were then reconstructed in a Sicilian Baroque style. Primarily for this reason, the city has been included, together with the surrounding territory as an area protected by the UNESCO World Heritage program. Since 1987, by a presidential decree, Caltanissetta was granted the status as a city and is about 70 kilometers (43 mi) southwest of Catania.

Piazza Armerina: The Villa Romana del Casale is a large and elaborate Roman villa or palace located about 3 km from the town of Piazza Armerina. Over the years the excavations have revealed one of the richest, largest, and varied collections of Roman mosaics in the entire world. The perfectly preserved floor of polychrome mosaics occupy 3,500 square meters and are the main attraction of the villa, which also included thermal baths, sumptuous rooms and colonnaded halls. Villa Romana was a lavish patrician residence built at the center of a huge agricultural estate at the end of the 4ᵗʰ century AD. It is in the remote southern Erei Mountains, at 697 meters above sea level, and is located just south of Enna, right in the center of Sicily, approximately 95 km southwest of Catania and 122 km northwest of Siracusa. The villa is thought to have belonged to a member of the Roman senatorial aristocracy who traded in exotic animals. The villa and its mosaics were abandoned for centuries and only rediscovered in the early 19ᵗʰ century. The mosaics are made of many different marble and glass chips, and are outstanding for their vivid colors and their craftsmanship, influenced by the North African culture. They depict hunting scenes, cupids fishing, chariot races, young female athletes in skimpy dresses, sagas of heroes and myths like Ulysses. Among the most famous and well-preserved mosaics are the so-called 'Bikini Girls', in the Chamber of the Ten Maidens, which portray young women dressed in what look like bikinis that apparently weren't invented in the 1950s like, it was assumed. The maidens are showed performing sports including weight-lifting, discus throwing, racing and ball games. The 'Little Hunt' mosaic show hunters using dogs and capturing a variety of game.

This historic place has been designated as a UNESCO World Heritage Site, inserted on the heritage list in 1997. It is recommended that visitors take some time to also visit the town of Piazza Armerina rather than limit the visit to the Villa. There are many other wonderful buildings in this historic town to visit including the 18ᵗʰ century Duomo, Cattedrale di Maria Santissima delle Vittorie, which dominates the town standing majestically on top of a hill. The massive Baroque cathedral was built on the 15ᵗʰ-century foundations of a former church, from which the bell tower was taken and reused. Also original to the 15ᵗʰ century church are the Catalan-Gothic style windows on the left side. The dome dates from 1768. The façade has a notable portal with spiral columns by Leonardo De Luca. The interior, with a single large nave, houses the Madonna delle Vittoria. The cathedral has an unusual two-sided crucifix by an unknown artist. The Diocesan Museum holds reliquaries, articles of silverware, monstrance and other religious art works.

Visiting the Villa Romana del Casale Romano is like being catapulted back into ancient Rome. Going through the numerous rooms and the long corridors of the villa, which was also declared a UNESCO World Heritage Site, is a majestic work of art in terms of size and value that delights tourists with its elegant mosaics spread over 3500 m2, whose paintings let one imagine how life was at the end of the third century AD.

Then there is the elegant town hall and grand old palazzi such as the Palazzo Trigona. For those who enjoy wandering through small streets and finding hidden places, try the 13th-century area round the Via Monte near the Duomo. It is recommended, if possible, that an authorized guide used for the visit. Every year, from 12 to 14 August, the Palio dei Normanni is held, a historical re-enactment of the Norman militias entering the entrance the ancient city of Plutia to free the Christian population from the yoke of the Saracens. The event takes place over the course of three days and involves about 600 people including ladies, notables, knights and Norman troops led by Count Roger the Norman, all of them parading through the city streets in Mediaeval costume. The highlight of the event is the Quintana, the exciting equestrian joust between the city's 4 districts that compete for the Palio.

Erice (Eryx): Still sits hidden in its cloud, just as Gene described in Roundabout. It is not be much different than when Gene and his new found friends (a Greek professor and his Swedish wife) "stepped into the damp obscurity of the public square." Be warned that as a result of the cloud it can be quite chilly, even in the Sicilian summer. As the wife of the Greek professor said, "one should see Erice whether one sees it or not." When we visited Erice, sure enough, it was covered by fog as it was on many of my subsequent visits. The town originated as a settlement was not a Greek colony, since the Phoenicians founded it, but was later largely Hellenized, fortified by the Phoenicians and conquered by the Carthaginians and then the Romans. Known in antiquity as Eryx, it was conquered by the Aghlabids in 831 and renamed Cebel Hamid and was ruled by the Arabs until the Norman Conquest in 1167. The Normans renamed it Monte San Giuliano, a name it maintained until 1934. It was famous throughout the Mediterranean for the temple of Venus Erycina. The influence of the Spanish culture is evident and just the last of many, starting with the Greek then the Saracen and finally, the Normans. The town of Erice is situated on top of Mount Erice at more than 750 meters above sea level. It has overlooked the coast below for thousands of years and has been considered a strategic point since the Trojan exiles made it their home for the first time. The medieval hamlet is accessible from Trapani by a twisty road or in alternative in modern time, by the panoramic cable car that in about 10 minutes takes you to the gate of the town. Once inside, the first thing you'll see will be the huge neo-gothic cathedral, dedicated to Mary of Assumption, with its 28-meters-high bell tower, one of approximately 60 churches, some in ruins. The town is surrounded by winegrowing cultures and full of history. This little town will surprise you with its breathtaking panorama and the enchanting 700 years old village. Perfect for its position and known for its beauty, Erice has always been a leading actor not only in the island's history but also in its mythology. Toby and I really enjoyed visiting this charming little town. The ancient Greek name of Erice was Eryx and its foundation was associated with the eponymous Greek hero Eryx. It was not a Greek colony, as the Phoenicians found it, but was largely Hellenized. It was destroyed in the First Punic War by the Carthaginians, and from then on declined in importance. Eryx was conquered by the Aghlebids in 831 and was renamed as Cebel Hamid (in Western sources Gebel Hamed, meaning Mountain of Hamid). It was ruled by the Arabs until the Norman Conquest of Sicily in 1167.

Cefalù: Is a coastal city in northern Sicily and has currently a population of 14,000. It is known for its Norman cathedral, a 12th century fortress-like structure with elaborate Byzantine mosaics and soaring twin towers. Nearby, the Mandralisca Museum is the home to archaeological exhibits and a picture galley with a portrait by Antonello da Messina. Cefalù is in a beautiful setting at the foot of a towering rock, halfway along the north coast of Sicily. The pretty little fishing harbor and the old town streets are dominated by the Norman Cathedral and, a long sandy beach right below the old town, has made Cefalù a popular holiday resort. The beautiful beaches of Mazzaforno and Settefrati lie to the west. And it is also a great place for camping, which my family and I really enjoyed.

Pachino: Pachino is a town and commune in the Province of Siracusa. It was founded in 1760 by the nobles Starraba, princes of Giardinelli and marquises of Rudini, The name derives from the Latin word Bacchus, which is the Roman god of wine, and the word vinum, which is the Latin word for wine. The population is approximately 22,500. The US Navy has a small radar base in Pachino that is serviced from NAF Sigonella that I often enjoyed visiting.

Selinunte and Segesta are the most ancient Greek settlements in Sicily. Segesta is a city located on Mount Barbaro and was the chief city of the Etymi, a people for whom Thucydides claimed to be of Trojan origin; However, the Greek culture influence seem to have been prominent in this trading city and emerged as one of the most important Siceliot (Sicilian–Greek) cities of antiquity. It was one of the major cities of the Elymians, one of the three indigenous peoples of Sicily. The temple of Segesta, located 13 kilometers from Selenunte, was built in late 5 BC when trade was at the height of its activity. Segesta is considered the best surviving example of Doric architecture in Europe. Segesta was one of the major cities of the Elymians, one of the three indigenous peoples of Sicily. The other major cities of the Elymians were Eryx and Entella. It is located in the northwestern part of Sicily near the modern commune of Calatafimi-Segesta in the province of Trapani.

The Doric order was one on three orders of Greek and Roman architecture, the other two are Ionic and the Corinthian. Currently work is continuing at the hilltop theater and the entire area is now protected by a fence that has been placed around the temple and the theater. A lot of restoration occurred at Selinunte since Bonner visited what he considered then "as a pile of rocks" has now been put together and designated as Temple E. Anyway, what has today remained in Selinunte and Segesta is absolutely worth seeing and admired. Selinunte and Segesta share nearly the same border and they only are at a distance of 30 kilometers from each other. The climb to the top of the hill has been facilitated by a road, or if one prefers, the comfort of a bus ride, that is provided on a regular basis for a small fee. There is also a small café/souvenir shop located in the valley between the temple and the theater so as to be both convenient and unobtrusive. Toby and I enjoyed visiting these two interesting sites.

Letojanni: Bonner usually visited Letojanni for its annual carnival and cultural and leisure time programs for all ages during the summer. Letojanni started out as a small fishing town called the "marina" for Gallodoro, the hillside town that was the primary center and habitation. The name "Letojanni" is said to derive from the Sicilian pronunciation of "lieti anni" meaning happy years. Nestled on the coast to the north of Taormina and Naxos, Letojanni is a popular coastal resort. The town outlines the gulf and enjoys year-round mild climate with abundant sunshine to warm the beaches and make the water of the sparkle. The beaches are a mix of fine sand and small pebbles and stretch down to

Naxos. The inauguration of the railroad and the modern highway opened up the previously isolated area and has attracted sun-seeking tourists. Letojanni enjoys a lively atmosphere with sun-filled piazzas, shop-lined streets, and plenty of cafes and restaurants one can taste the regions sea food specialties. The church of San Giuseppe, which was built in neurotic style with a bell tower and a round Romanesque-like rose window. There are lovely mosaics inside and a decorative balustrade outside. The first Sunday of August celebrates San Giuseppe, the patron saint with a sea-going procession that carries the statue of the saint on a boat. As the most evocative and awaited Feast of San Giuseppe (Joseph) which draws all the faithful to celebrate the patron saint of the city.

Tindari: Is a town of Greek origin on the northern coast of Sicily, west of Messina and east of Patti and is best known for its principle church known as the Tindari Sanctuary and the archaeological site of the ancient city. The original city was built from the 4th century BC and survived until the 8th century. It suffered a great deal when part of a cliff collapsed and some of the town fell into the sea in the 1st century and again, when an earthquake hit the region in the 4th century. From Tindari there are wonderful views of the sea and the Aeolian Islands. Throughout its history Tindari has been Greek, Carthaginian, Roman, Byzantine and Arab and various monuments remain from those times but the most visited site here is the Tindari Sanctuary which can be seen balancing on the edge of the cliff as seen from the Palermo-Messina autostrada (motorway), and is on the edge of the main square in the town. Inside the sanctuary is the statue of the "Black Madonna", a wooden sculpture perhaps from Syria or Egypt where it was carved around the 12th century. There are various legends relating to its arrival in Tindari and it now sits behind the altar with the inscription "I am black but am beautiful". The Black Madonna is an important Tindari tourist attraction as well as for religious pilgrimages. The Sanctuary of the Black Madonna is the

most significant monuments in the ancient part of "Tyndaris", as
the town was known. The basilica is thought to have been built
in the early Roman Empire. Originally it was the "gymnasium",
where gymnastic exercises took place, after which it is thought that
it might have been a market or a place of worship. The other major
monument in Tindari archaeological park is the theatre, built in
Greek times between the end of the 4th and 3rd centuries BC, and
which could hold about 3,000 people. The name Tyndaris is of
mythological origin and stems from that of legendary Greek leader
Tyndareus. Bonner describes his visit where he took a train from
Messina, riding third class together with locals and their livestock.
He got off in the town of Oliveri. There he took a footpath up the
mountainside to the high-lying road that passes close to Tindari,
some four mile distance. He really enjoyed visiting this area.

Phoenicia was an ancient civilization in Canaan which
covered most of the western coastal part of the Fertile Crescent
once considered the "cradle of civilization." The Fertile Crescent's
place among the Tigris, Euphrates and the Nile rivers once led to an
abundance of riches. Now the depletion of those resources has led
to strife in the Middle East. Several major Phoenician cities were
built on the coastline of the Mediterranean. It was an enterprising
maritime trading culture that spread across the Mediterranean
from 1550 BC to 300 BC. They established colonies in Sicily and
North Africa where the great trading city of Carthage became
famous as one of Ancient Rome's most formidable foes, and as far
west as Spain (the port of Cadiz is the ancient Phoenician city of
Gases). Their homeland was dry and not suitable for farming, so
the Phoenicians turned to the sea to become the greatest travelers
and traders of their time. They were the first Mediterranean
people to venture beyond the Strait of Gibraltar. Some scholars
believe that the Phoenicians traded for tin with inhabitants of the
southern coast of Britain. Some evidence exists for an even more
remarkable feat—sailing around the continent of Africa by way

of the Red Sea and back through the Strait of Gibraltar. Such a trip was not repeated again for 2,000 years. The Greek historian Herodotus relates this achievement. Cyrus the Great conquered Phoenicia in 539 BC. The Persians divided Phoenicia into four vassal kingdoms. They prospered, furnishing fleets for the Persian kings. Phoenician influence declined after this. It is likely that much of the Phoenician population migrated to Carthage and other colonies following the Persian conquest. In 350 or 345 BC a rebellion in Sidon led by Tennes was crushed by Artaxerxes III. Phoenicians, Greeks, Romans, Saracens, and Normans – nearly 3000 years of recorded history – the mysterious spell cast upon races, people, and individuals by this Mediterranean island has been proverbial. It is the curious blend of Pagan and Christian, the elbowing of grandeur by the commonplace, with which one is constantly confronted in everyday life that constitutes one of Sicily's most irreversible charms.

Chapter 19

Sicilian Roundabout can be considered a different kind of guide book. For it is mainly, as its title implies, a purely Bonner's personal record of places he visited, or revisited, since World War two, together with some historical notes and a few random reminiscences of historical notes of the author's earlier travels in this fabled land. And throughout the book there are thumbnail sketches of colorful personalities and diverting incidents. It was a winter spent in Sicily, immediately preceding the First World War that awakened Eugene Bonner's interest in the place and its people, its myths, legends and history. His interest strengthened and perpetuated by long periods of intermittent residence in Taormina. Apart from the fact that the author found "the urge to write about Sicily too strong to resist" he was no less eager to correct the erroneous impression, current among an uninformed minority immediately after World War II, that the island itself had been reduced to a mass of ruins. Nothing in the story of Sicily with myth and legend, and so real could have been more ludicrously and entirely untrue as Mr. Bonner points out: "for it is a little short of miraculous how very few of the great works of antiquity, famous buildings and places of historical interest were even touched". Among those which were damaged, most have since been completely and meticulously restored to their former state. In addition to which, he has taken great pains to enlarge upon the incredible and universal advances which have been made in Sicily. So bound up in the story of Sicily with myth and legend, and so real seeming, even today, are the fabulous beings that antique world where gods, demigods, and titans walked with living men, that is not always easy to disentangle the factual from the legendary. What mortal woman in Sicilian history are as real to us as Persephone and Ceres; what flesh and blood men (though the males fare a bit better) are as well-known as Pluto and Ulysses? What earthly, or unearthly, chance has Timoleon of Syracuse against Hercules, or Constance of Aragon against Arethusa? As a matter of fact, the recorded history of Sicily yields little or nothing in romantic interest to its mythology. Reaching backward as it does, some three thousand years, into the past and crowed as it is with tales of great events and heroic personalities as multitudinous and involved as to be well night bewildering, it composes one of the most stupendous epics in all literature. For the serious student of antiquity there exists a wealth of authentic material (much of it in English or English translation) ranging from the ancient Greek and Roman chronicles to historical works of our own era and students may be referred to these writings. The Sicily one sees today is an essentially a "Latin" region which, as part of Italy, has a distinct yet Italian character. For the most part, the people are Roman Catholic (at least nominally) and superficially those of Palermo and Catania don't seem too different from those of Naples or southern Italy. The unification of Spain led to a degree of stability and forged a powerful European state prepared to defend its interests, both in Europe and in the emerging New World colonies. Sicily, however, was essentially a Spanish "possession." Dynastically, the rulers of Aragon and then all Spain occasionally controlled not only Sicily but much of southern Italy (the Kingdom of Naples). Several, including the remarkable Charles V, were Hapsburgs who ruled not only Spain and her possessions but also Austria and various lands of central Europe. This period lasted for over two hundred years, until the War of the Spanish Succession and the brief reign (1713-1720) of Vittorio Amadeo of Savoy.

Sicilian puppets or Pupi Siciliani: Also called marionettes are armed puppets that date back to the popular epic theater of the nineteenth century, which developed and spread in Naples, Rome and then in Sicily, where it reached its maximum splendor. The puppet theatre known as the "Opera dei Pupi" emerged in Sicily at the beginning of the nineteenth century and enjoyed great success among the island's working classes. Sicilian Marionettes theaters (Opra d'ipuppi), Bonner notes, are almost, at least were, as plentiful in Sicily as movie houses in the United States. These theaters were, until recent times, the most popular form of entertainment in Sicily. The largest cities, like Palermo, Catania, and Messina had permanent puppet theaters that were located, as a rule, in the more populous and less affluent neighborhoods of the cities. Smaller towns were visited by traveling puppeteers who set up stages in unused stables, sheds, other available vacant buildings, and outdoors in the town squares (piazzas). My entire family, especially my daughters, enjoyed seeing some of these performances when they came to our town of Motta Sant Anastasia and when we went to Acireale and Catania to see performances in a permanent theater. We had the pleasure of seeing these varied performances many times.

The puppeteers were and are very skillful and very entertaining. My children, their friends as well as the adults all enjoyed the shows. The puppeteers tell stories based on medieval chivalric literature and other sources, such as Italian poems of the Renaissance, the lives of saints and tales of notorious bandits. The dialogues in these performances are largely improvised by the puppeteers. The two main Sicilian puppet schools in Palermo and Catania were distinguished principally by the size and shape of the puppets, the operating techniques and the variety of colorful stage backdrops. These theatres were often family-run businesses; the carving, painting and construction of the puppets, renowned for their intense expressions, were carried out by craftspeople employing traditional methods. The puppeteers constantly endeavored to outdo each other with their shows, and they exerted great influence over their audience. In the past, these performances took place over several evenings and provided opportunities for social gatherings. The economic and social upheavals caused by the extraordinary economic boom in Italy of the 1950s had a considerable negative effect on the tradition, threatening its very foundations. The Opera dei Pupi is the only example of an uninterrupted tradition of this type of theatre.

The Normans: Were a population arising in the medieval Duchy of Normandy from the intermingling between Norse Viking settlers and indigenous West Franks and Gallo-Romans. The term is also used to denote emigrants from the duchy who conquered other territories such as England and Sicily. The Norman conquest of Sicily began in 1061 when Roger de Hauteville and his brother Robert de Guiscard crossed the strait from Calabria and with only a handful of men seized Messina. Thirty years later they had driven out the Saracens and were in control of the whole island. The Sicily of Roger II and his successors, William I and William II, became a meeting place of cultures. Roger II built churches and castles all along the northern coast of Sicily, but by far his finest achievement is the royal chapel, the Cappella Palatina, in the Norman palace in Palermo. One of the most beautiful features of the Palatine chapel is the wooden Saracenic ceiling, which is of Islamic inspiration. Islamic architecture is one of the world's most celebrated building traditions. Known for its radiant colors, rich patterns, and symmetrical silhouettes, this distinctive approach has been popular in the Muslim world since the 7th century. It was a remarkable period of tolerance, from 1072 until 1194, in which the arts flourished and the city of Palermo, which in the 11th century counted more than 300,000 inhabitants, became the center of the Norman court in all of Europe and one of the most important international centers of trade between east and west. Greek, French, Latin and Arabic were spoken at court; Latin translations of Greek and Arab classics were made; Roger had an astrological observatory installed in his palace.

Mount Etna, or simply Etna is a very active volcano on the east coast of Sicily between the cities of Messina and Catania. A picture that I took of Etna from where I worked at NAS Sigonella.

I witnessed the eruptions of Mt Etna during our 12 wonderful years living and working in Sicily and in my many visits to the island when I was at the US Embassy in Rome and was responsible to coordinate re-construction of NAS Sigonella with the Italian government and Italian military. I really enjoyed witnessing so many spectacular eruptions. Mt Etna is one of the tallest active volcanoes in Europe and the tallest peak in Italy south of the Alps. The current height is approximately, 3,357 meters. Over a six-month period in 2021, Etna erupted so much volcanic material that its height increased by approximately 100 feet. It is by far the largest of the three active volcanoes in Italy, being about two and a half times the height of the next largest, Mount Vesuvius, near Naples (that has not had an active eruption since World War 2). The fertile volcanic soils support extensive agriculture, orchards with vineyards and agricultural fields spread across the lower slopes of the mountain and the broad Plain of Catania to the south where we lived. The fertile soil and the mild Sicilian weather, allows farmers to harvest two crops a year. Due to its history of recent activity and nearby population, Mount Etna has been designated a "Decade Volcano" by the United Nations. Decade Volcanoes are 16 volcanos identified by the International Association of Volcanology and Chemistry of the Earth's Inferior (IAVCET) as being worthy of particular study in light of their history of large, destructive eruptions and proximity to densely populated areas. A volcano may be designated a Decade Volcano if it exhibits more than one volcanic hazard and shows recent geological activity, is located in a densely populated area is physically accessible for study and, most important, there is local support for the work. Volcanic activity first took place at Etna about 500,000 years ago, with eruptions occurring beneath the sea off the ancient coastline of Sicily. The most recent event is thought to have occurred about 2,000 years ago, forming what is known as the Piano Caldera. This caldera has been almost entirely filled by subsequent lava flow but is still visible as a distinct break in the slope of the mountain near the base of the present-day summit cone. The 1669 eruption was Etna's most destructive since 122 BCE, it started on 11 March 1669 and produced lava flows that destroyed at least 10 villages on its southern slope before reaching the walls of the city of Catania, five weeks later, on 15 April. Fortunately, the lava was largely diverted by the walls surrounding the city, into the sea to the south of the city, filling the harbor of Catania. A small portion of lava eventually broke through a fragile section of the city walls on the western side of Catania and destroyed a few buildings before stopping in the rear of the Benedictine monastery, without reaching the center of the city (considered by some a miracle). Other major 20th-century eruptions occurred in 1949, 1971, 1979, 1981, 1983 and 1991–1993. In the1971 eruption, which I witnessed, lava buried the Etna Observatory, which had been built in the late 19th century, also destroyed the first generation of the Etna cable-car, and seriously threatened several small villages on Etna's east flank. In March 1981, the town of Randazzo on the northwestern flank of Etna narrowly escaped destruction by unusually fast-moving lava flows. That eruption was remarkably similar to one in 1928 that destroyed Mascali. The 1991–1993 eruptions saw the town of Zafferana threatened by a lava flow, but successful diversion efforts saved the town with the loss of only one building a few hundred meters from the town's margin. For six years (1995–2001) it was an unusually intense activity at the four summit craters of Etna, which involved activity from seven distinct eruptive fissures, mostly on the south slope of the volcano. This activity was well covered by the mass-media because it occurred at the height of the tourist season and numerous reporters and journalists were in Italy to cover the G8 summit in Genoa. I happened to be in Genova at the same time to support of the US delegation. It also occurred close to one of the popular tourist areas, and thus was easily accessible. Part of the "Etna Sud" tourist area, including the arrival station of the

Etna cable car, were damaged by this eruption, which otherwise was a rather modest-sized event by Etna standards. In 2002–2003, a much larger eruptions threw up a huge column of ash that could easily be seen from space and fell as far away as Libya. The eruption also completely destroyed the tourist station Piano Provenzana, on the northeastern flank of the volcano, and part of the tourist station "Etna Sud" around the Rifugio Sapienza on the south flank. The Rifugio Sapienza is near the site of a cable car station which had been destroyed in the 1983 eruption and had been recently rebuilt. An eruption on the morning of 13 May 2008, immediately to the east of Etna's summit craters was accompanied by a swarm of more than 200 earthquakes and significant ground deformation in the summit area. The eruption continued at a slowly diminishing rate for 417 days, until 6 July 2009. Through January 2011 to February 2012, the summit craters of Etna were the site of intense activity. Frequent eruptions and ash columns forced the authorities to shut down the Catania airport on several occasions. The July 2011 episode also endangered the Sapienza Refuge, the main tourist hub on the volcano, but the lava flow was successfully diverted. On 3 December 2015 an eruption occurred which climaxed between 03:20 and 04:10 local time. The voragine or crater exhibited a lava fountain which reached 1 km in height, with an ash plume which reached 3 km in height. The activity continued on the following days, with an ash plume that reached 7 km in height that forced Catania airport to shut down again for a few hours. While living in Sicily many times our town was covered by fine ash. An eruption on 16 March 2017 injured 10 people, including a BBC News television crew, after magma exploded upon contact with snow.

An eruption on 24 December 2018 at shallow depth, spewed ash into the air, forcing the closure of airspace around Mount Etna. Two days later, a magnitude 4.9 earthquake shook the town of Fleri and surrounding towns and hamlets in the Province of Catania, damaging buildings and injuring four people. Beginning in February 2021, Mount Etna began a series of explosive eruptions, which have had an impact on nearby villages and cities, with volcanic ash and rock falling as far away as Catania. As of 12 March 2021, the volcano has erupted 11 times in three weeks. The eruptions have consistently sent ash clouds over 10 km into the air, closing on several occasions Sicilian airports, especially Fontarossa airport in Catania as well as the Sigonella military airport. There were no reports of injuries at the time. The most recent major eruption occurred on 11 February 2022 and continued for several days. Mt Etna for sure has not disappointed volcano watchers. There is an interesting train service available called the Circumetnea train that almost entirely encircles Mount Etna, travelling down a narrow-gauge railway. It is a great train ride which my family and I took on several occasions, giving passengers the opportunity to see Mt Etna from all angles.

Chapter 20

Toby and I had a great time visiting some many historical places on the island that we were familiar with most but continued to learn more history of this beautiful island. To support the US Navy military operations, I visited the US Navy base at Sigonella, Sicily many times when I worked at the US Embassy in Rome from1993 until I retired in 2006. On these visits I spend time with my friends in Motta Sant Anastasia and Catania and took some trips around the island and learned to appreciate it even more. In 2000 Toby and his wife Martha visited me in Rome and we took a trip to Catania and attended a Catania soccer game. To the delight of many fans, we hung our flag in the stands as discussed and pictured in the preface. Although it had been almost 30 years since we first hung the banner at the stadium, (as pictured in the introduction) many of the fans remembered us and the flag, we received a standing ovation. It was a great time to be with Toby and go back to the Cibali.

NAS Sigonella: I was stationed at the United States Naval Air Facility (NAF), Sigonella, Sicily from 1963 to 1976 with a one year break in 1966 when I served on the USS Bushnell in Key West, FL and Charleston, SC. At Sigonella I served for almost 5 years on US Navy active duty, and seven years as a US Civil Servant. My family and I really enjoyed and loved Sicily and the Sicilians as I discussed above. NAF Sigonella was formally established 15 June 1959. The facility was conceived in the early 1950s when the

U.S. Navy P2V Neptune planes began to outgrow their facility at Hal Far base on the small island nation of Malta. When there was limited room for expansion at the Malta base plans to move operations to Italy began. The U.S. Navy obtained NATO backing to be hosted in Italy, more specifically on the island of Sicily. Italy made the land available under a temporary agreement signed 25 June 1957. Six days later, the Landing Ship Tank (LSTs) began to deliver equipment from the Malta base to Sicily. Ground was broken in September 1957, and construction on the administrative area, later named NAF I, was started in 1958. The facility was built on top of a World War Two airfield where fighters and bombers of the German Air Force had operated during the Second World War. In fact, traces of the German planes and equipment were found for many years. In late 1985 work crews, belonging to NMCB 133, were repairing and installing sidewalks in the housing area at NAF I when they uncovered a small stockpile of Luftwaffe antiaircraft ammunition. The stockpile had apparently belonged to an antiaircraft position that had been buried during raids in the Allied invasion of 1943. When I was stationed at Sigonella some bombs were uncovered what had become a the Sigonella golf course The first Americans arrived for work at the future base in March 1957 when there were no buildings so the Americans worked for up to six months in a large warehouse complex in the city of Catania opposite the city's cemetery on the right side of the street as one enters the city from the base. By the end of August 1959, the airfield, named NAF II was available for daylight flights under visual flight rules (VFR). Twenty four flights were logged by 31 August. The airport resides at an elevation of 79 feet above sea level. It has two asphalt paved runways: 10R/28L which measures 8,077 feet × 148 feet and 10L/28R measuring 8,012 feet × 92 feet. One of Sigonella's first buildings was used by the Army Corps of Engineers for their offices, later sharing it with Special Services, or what is now called Morale, Welfare and Recreation

(MWR). Around 1966, the Armed Forces Network (AFN) came to Sigonella and initially shared the facility with Special Services, which soon after moved out, leaving the building for exclusive use by the broadcasters. In 1965 the Italian Air Force established their 41st Antisubmarine Warfare Wing (86st and 88st Gruppo) with mixed crews from the Italian Air Force and Italian Navy at Sigonella NAF II. In the 1980s, "Naval Air Facility (NAF)" Sigonella was renamed as a "Naval Air Station (NAS)".

The Achille Lauro incident: The Achille Lauro hijacking took place on 7 October 1985 when the Italian liner was taken over by four men representing the Palestinian Liberation Front (PLF) off the coast of Egypt as she was sailing from Alexandria, Egypt to Ashdod, Israel. Tragically, a 69-year-old Jewish American man in a wheelchair, Leon Klinghoffer, was murdered by the hijackers and thrown overboard. The hijacking sparked what became known as the "Sigonella Crisis." On the night of 10 October 1985, there were some very tense and potentially dangerous hours on NAS II when the Italian Carabinieri (national police), working with the Italian Air Force, faced off with the US Army's Delta Force and came close to firing upon one another. The US F-14s had intercepted and instructed the Egyptian Boeing 737 passenger airliner carrying the hijackers to land at the NATO base of Sigonella where the Americans had planned to take the hijackers into custody. Italy had been informed of the US maneuver only minutes before because the United States hoped to gain custody of the hijackers. A tense standoff ensued between U.S. and Italian forces. The Italian Prime Minister Bettino Craxi insisted that the hijackers were on Italian territory (and they clearly were) and therefore under Italian jurisdiction. The Italian authorities therefore refused to allow the US Navy SEALs to board the plane, threatening to open fire on the Americans had they made an attempt to do so. The ensuing tense stand-off lasted throughout the night. I remember that incident well and I was very concerned for our relationship with the Italian military and government that had been excellent until this incident. It also became clear that NAS II was an Italian military installation not a US base as many Americans had erroneously assumed. Thankfully, President Ronald Reagan gave the order for the Americans to stand down. The hijackers were taken off the airplane and arrested by the Italian Carabinieri and eventually tried and sentenced by an Italian court and jailed in Italy. The friendly relations between US and Italian military quickly returned to normal.

On 1 April 2004, the Defense Logistics Agency (DLA) opened Defense Depot Sigonella Italy on NAS II to serve as a supply base for the Mediterranean. DLA also provides fuel and US property disposal from NAS Sigonella. When NATO took the military intervention in Libya in 2011, NAS Sigonella played an important role in US Operation Odyssey Dawn because of its short distance to that country. As Libya remained unstable in 2013, a Special Purpose Marine Air Ground Task Force–Crisis Response unit was formed and an element of this was moved to Sigonella to be within V–22 range of Libya.

As discussed above, construction of the base was authorized by the Italian government, following an agreement between the US and the Italian governments, signed 25 June 1957. The base became fully operational in 1959. I was first stationed at Sigonella on December 1963 as a young hospital corpsman, X–Ray technician. I had the honor of serving for 12 years at Sigonella, 5 years on active duty and 7 years a Civil Servant. Of course I was honored to be invited to attend the 50th anniversary celebration held on the base on June 12 2009. It was a great ceremony that brought back many pleasant memories of my time at Sigonella. Also in attendance were many civilians who had worked on the base during my time there. It was a pleasure seeing so many folks I had served with over the years. Some pictures of the event and a recent picture of the front gate of NAS Sigonella, a very strategic base that I consider the most important US Base of the US Europeans command.

My family and I really enjoyed our time in Sicily and having so many wonderful memories as well as many Sicilian friends, they were just great. Sicily had some very good TV and movie personalities that we enjoyed watching over the years. One of the most famous was the comedy due of Franco and Ciccio who were Italian actors Franco Franchi and Ciccio Ingrassia, they were very popular in the 1960s and 1970s. On my return to the United States I attended a dinner and had the pleasure of meeting one of the due, Franco Franchi.

Chapter 21

I have discussed my life in my first book "my life story" so I will try not be too repetitive but I wanted to include some points of interest in this book. I was fortunate to serve in Sicily in the military and as a civil servant for about 12 years. Since all good things must come to an end, my overseas assignment came to an end and in 1977 and I was transferred to the Transportation office, Naval Air Warfare Center, Warminster, PA. It was a big change and I did not adapt well. For starters, I had received priority placement to this supervisory position which had been promised to the most senior member of the existing staff of that office. This did not go down well with the all-female staff and even my immediate supervisor, and I didn't blame them. I did not enjoy the assignment but fortunately a friend of mine, Frank Pallone from US Navy Headquarters informed me there was a position at Military Traffic Management Command (MTMC) in Washington, DC for which I was qualified and suggested I apply.

The position came with a promotion to GS-11and a job that really interested me, so I applied and was hired. Since at the time I had a wife and three daughters and had just purchased a home in Warminster, I could not afford to try to sell the house I had recently purchased and move the family to Washington, DC. We decided for the family to remain in Warminster and for me to rent a room in DC and go home most weekends. I also decided to re-register and attend the University of Maryland Pentagon campus four evenings a week and continue to work on a BS degree from that university. Since I remained eligible for the GI bill, the tuition was covered plus I received approximately $300.00 a month – a good deal. I reported to MTMC and began my new job which was to assist transportation offices at all US military bases in the world, including my former bases at Warminster, Sigonella and Naples. My main responsibility was to assist transportation officers to deal with military entitlements for service members and their families and to ensure that moving companies provided acceptable service. It was a very interesting and challenging position which I really enjoyed. The job and going for a 3 hour evening college courses after work at the Pentagon kept me, to say the least, very busy.

Although busy with work and college and missing my family I still enjoyed this interesting position and living in our historic nation's capital. I was in daily contact with transportations offices in the US as well as overseas and provided them assistance. In spite of being so busy working and going to college, as noted above, I enjoyed both my job and attending University of Maryland Pentagon campus. After two years in DC I completed the course requirements and obtained a Bachelor Degree (BS) in Business Administration. I worked hard and was proud of my achievement as was my family. Not bad for a poor immigrant, high school dropout. As noted above, I had a great graduation ceremony at the campus of the University of Maryland (my first time on the campus itself) and was very happy that my family, including my mom attended. Of course, being from an immigrant family I was and remain very proud to graduate from college. I posted so many pictures above in my cap and gown because I was and remain very proud of this accomplishment at age 38. This is another picture of me at the graduation. In spite of having learned English only in my teens, dropping out of high school, married very young with a family and working full-time, thanks to the GI Bill I did get my degree.

I had been in DC for over 2 years and decided it was time
to have my family join me and began looking for an affordable
house to buy and move my family. While working at MTMC I
resolved many operational problems for the Transportation Offices,
including the one in Naples and frequently spoke to the Officer in
charge of that office. During one conversation he asked if I would
be interested in a supervisory position in that troubled office. If I
was, he could arrange for me to be hired. Of course I accepted the
offer and soon received orders to report to the US Naval Support
Activity in Naples. My wife was thrilled my two older daughters,
now in their late teens, not so much. They had a good social life
and many friends in the area. With a little coxing and a promise
they could return to the US in a year if they wanted, they decided
to join us. We were fortunate to sell our home with no problem,
have our furniture packed up and shipped to Italy. In November
1979 we arrived in Naples. My three daughters quickly adapted
since they spoke Italian and were familiar with the Italian culture.
In Naples I was the Supply Department, Transportation Officer

and really enjoyed my job and working with Italian employees and moving companies. We spent five years in Naples where my oldest daughter Eva met and married a US Air Force officer, Emerick Aulicino. They were married in very nice ceremony in Saint Peter Basilica in the Vatican, a very beautiful setting.

Following the ceremony we drove to San Marino for a great reception for our friends and relatives at the Ristorante Rossi. After five great years in Naples in charge of moving service member's personal effects and arranging transportation for members and their families, I was to return to my previous job at MTMC in

Washington as per civil service policy. As I was preparing to return to DC, I received a call from a friend who informed me that there was a vacancy at the US Army base at Camp Darby near Pisa for a position for which I was somewhat qualified since the most important qualification was knowledge of the Italian language and if I was interested he could arrange for me to get a position. I accepted the offer and moved with my family, now down to 4, to Tirrenia, a town near Pisa. It was an interesting assignment being in charge of a mechanical shop responsible for repairing and preparing for long-term storage military equipment. It was a great learning experience for me. I had about 20 skilled Italian employees who taught me a lot about repairing and maintaining equipment. I was hired for this supervisory position mostly because of my language skills which came in very handy in dealing with the employees who did not speak English and I got along well with all of them and they really did a great job for me. While at Camp Darby my second oldest daughter Jacqueline, was married to Mike DeBoni, a JAG (lawyer) officer she had met in Naples. We had a great ceremony in San Marino followed by very nice reception in the same Rossi restaurant that we celebrated Eva's wedding. Mike and Jackie's friends from Naples as well as all my relatives in San Marino attended a great reception.

After three years at Camp Darby I received a call from Ed a friend who offered me a job at the US Army base at Vicenza. It came with a promotion to GS-12 and training in automation. I accepted the job and moved my family, now down 3, to the Vicenza area. As I discussed above, one of my best friends in Sicily was a soccer player, a goalie who played on the Catania team, Gigi Muraro who, as discussed above, we became good friends with the entire family during our time in Sicily. In Sicily Gigi Muraro and family rented apartments in the same compound and we became close friends and neighbors. His son Mirko, as discussed above, spent a lot of time with us and was very close to my one of my daughters, Christina. It was a very interesting job with a promotion and it was also great living near old friends in Dueville, a town near Vicenza. The job was also very interesting and although automation was a new field for me I enjoyed the work. Fortunately for me one of the other employee and my co-worker was a computer expert and he really helped me learn the basics of automation and I will be forever grateful for his technical assistance and friendship, he was a great teacher and I appreciated his guidance. His name is Ed Jakeobs, and we became great friends.

After two years working in automation I was offered and accepted another job in an area which, thankfully was more familiar to me, dealing with base operations to include coordinating transportation of household goods and overseeing operation of messing facilities. I really enjoyed this great job which involved frequent visits to my former base, at Campo Darby and travel to Greece and Turkey to assist them in base operations.

Pat and I and our daughter Christina also enjoyed living in Dueville and spending a lot of time with our dear friends the Muraros and having visits from our two married daughters. After five years at Vicenza I was notified that I had been overseas well in excess of the five year Civil Service overseas limitation for career civilians, in fact I had been in Italy for 13 consecutive years. I was informed that I had to register for a priority placement in a similar position in the US and had to accept the first offer and a transfer when there was such a vacancy. Although disappointed, I felt very fortunate for having had the opportunity to serve my country overseas for so many years and had no complaints in having to return to a similar position in the US. As I was preparing to be transferred to the US, a friend called me and told of an interesting position that had become available at the US Embassy in Rome for which I was qualified. The position was that of the Host Nation Liaison Officer which required Italian language skills and knowledge of US military operations in Italy. Since I had both, I applied and went to Rome for an interview. Following the interview I was offered the position on the spot which I accepted. I really enjoyed this interesting job and working with a group of skilled military and civilians in the Host Nation office of the US Embassy in Rome. I have included a group picture of the staff of my office in front of the Rome US Embassy.

In addition to being a very interesting position it came with a promotion to GS-13 and no overseas time limit. My wife was thrilled to move to Rome. It was a great job in a wonderful city and I really enjoyed having daily contact with senior Italian government and military officials. I also enjoyed working with all the US operated military bases in Italy and I frequently visited all the bases. I especially enjoyed visiting my first duty station in Italy, the Naval Air Facility, at Sigonella, Sicily that was undergoing expansion and construction of new facilities, which I oversaw. While at the embassy I was frequently assigned the duty of hosting senior US officials, like senators and congressmen. One of my

favorites with whom I spent many days together was Sen Bob
Dole. In 1994 I escorted him to Castel d'Aiano where he had been
wounded during World War 2. The folks there were overjoyed
to welcome him back for one of his many visits. They had a nice
lunch in his honor and he took part in a wreath laying ceremony.
We also took part in a US Veteran parade in a nearby town. Sen
Dole really enjoyed the visit as did I.

The same year I also escorted Sen Daniel Inouye and Sen
George Mc Govern. I really enjoyed their company and it was a
pleasure spending time with individuals whom I considered real
war heroes. I found all three to be very down to earth and just
good people. I also escorted many other US dignitaries, including
President George W. Bush and I enjoyed taking them around
Rome and having them meet Italian senior military and dignitaries
and interpreting for them.

It was a wonderful 14 years living and working in the eternal city and I did consider myself lucky to have had this great opportunity. While serving in Rome, one of my daughters, Jacqueline was diagnosed with Multiple Scoliosis (MS). As she was getting weaker she expressed the desire to visit Rome while she could still walk. She visited in 1979 and had the pleasure of meeting Pope John Pal II.

After 14 years in Rome I reluctantly retired and returned to the United States. While I was serving in Rome, Jacqueline MS had progressed to the point where she needed assistance to just function. After retiring and joined my wife in Goshen, IN Jackie frequently expressed the desire to visit Italy where she had lived for so many years. My wife and I and her husband decided to make her wish a reality since her health was declining. We made arrangements and my wife and I took Jackie to Italy, more specifically, my native country, San Marino. In 2006 we spent four months there where she received excellent medical care as well as physical therapy and her health improved. Also my many relatives and friends in San Marino and Italy visited frequently and also invited us to their homes for lunch or dinner. They all made a big fuss over Jackie and she really enjoyed all the attention. A couple of times a month we attended an MS dinners with her great Physical Therapist, Elia Bertoglio, her Neurologist Dr. Susanna Guttmann and about 30 individuals who, like Jackie, had MS. She really enjoyed these dinners and, although she was in worse shape than the others, she was always the most upbeat and enjoyed the dinners. On our return to the US her family and doctor were amazed at her improved condition and her positive attitude. Jackie expressed the desire to return to San Marino for another visit and to continue with the excellent medical care she had received. With her husband's support, I took her back a couple of months after our return to the US. She was thrilled to go back as were all of our relatives and friends and her doctor in San Marino who loved her. For 18 months Jackie and I lived in San Marino in the small but adequate apartment I had rented. Jackie required continuous care and had to be assisted in everything, including being fed. Although it was not easy, I enjoyed taking good care of her and she often expressed her appreciation. I had professional care givers visit daily to give her a morning shower and provide other specialized assistance. This time Jackie and I spent a lot of time traveling all over Italy to visit friends, including a visit to Sicily where she had lived for14 years. My wife Pat joined us in Sicily and we had a great time with the Schillaci family. When we visited Rome we stayed at a pensione (hotel) administered by mostly Polish nuns. The nuns were wonderful and took good care of Jackie and made her feel special.

Jackie and I also visited Our Lady of Lourdes shrine in France where Mary, the mother of Jesus, is venerated due to her apparitions that is believed by Roman Catholics to have occurred. The first apparition is believed to have happen on 11 February 1858 when Bernadette Soubirous was 14 years old. She told her mother that a "Lady" spoke to her in the cave of Massabielle while she was gathering firewood with her sister and a friend. The image of Our Lady of Lourdes has been widely copied and reproduced in shrines and homes, often in garden landscapes all over the world. Bernadette Soubirous was canonized by Pope Pius XI in 1933. Jackie and I really enjoyed our 5 day visit.

Following her 18 month stay with me in San Marino and Italy, I took Jackie back home to her family in Goshen. Although she really enjoyed her stay in Italy and San Marino she was very happy to be back with her family and her mother who, along with and her family a caregiver, took good care of her. I am very happy I was able to bring some happiness in her life. She passed away on July 26, 2017. She was an inspiration to me and I really do miss her I will never forget my Jackie.

For many years after Jackie returned to the US I spent about 3 months a year in San Marino where I had kept the same small apartment. In the summers I spent more than a month in Verona where I assisted a friend with a music class she was teaching. I provided transportation and assisted students, with translation and other assistance, as required.

I was really enjoying retirement, especially my yearly visits to Italy and San Marino, when about 7 years ago I became very ill and was taken to the Goshen hospital emergency room and then transferred to Elkhart General Hospital for emergency heart surgery. The surgery lasted several hours and it was touch and go. Following the first surgery I had another two heart surgeries within a week. It was a rough time that I barely survived. In fact I had the "The Last Rites" administered to me although I don't remember. The last rites is the celebration for those about to die when a person receives the Body and Blood of Christ. This is a special Catholic Eucharistic service celebrated near the time of death. I had my entire family around me and that, I believe, helped me survive. After several weeks of rehabilitation at a specialized facility, I regained my strength and returned home. Unfortunately a few months later I had to be taken to the hospital for another emergency heart surgery. This time I recovered quickly and was able to travel. As soon as I could I returned to San Marino and visited Rome. In Rome I was taken to the Vatican for the Pope's Wednesday audience. I was fortunate that the Pope come to me and blessed me. It was, to say the least, a great honor. It was honored to meet Pope Francis on other occasions.

I also met John Paul on several occasions including when Jackie and I were invited to shake his hand when Jackie could still walk.

Everything was going well and I was enjoying my visits to San Marino and Italy but a few years later I began to have some circulation problems and have been advised by my great cardiologist, Dr. Walter H. Halloran, to stay close to home and not travel overseas. I am fortunate to have a daughter, Christina who is a skilled nurse and takes good care of me. Although not being able to travel is disappointing, I cannot complain since I had, after a rough start in life being born during WW2, a decent life with many great friends, career opportunities not available to everyone and, most of all, an outstanding family to include, in addition to my wife and three daughters, nine grandchildren and now also four great grandchildren and looking forward to more. Also, I had great parents and have a great brother and sister and their families.

My sister Rita and brother Marino

I enjoyed traveling to many countries for work and pleasure. I have been very lucky and for that I will always be grateful.

My life and 47 year US government career – I was lucky

1941	Born, Republic of San Marino, 6 months after Pearl Harbor
1953	Emigrated to Detroit, Michigan/ 53-54 Struggled to lean English
1959	Dropped out of high school and joined the US Navy
1959	**Became a US Citizen**
59-60	US Navy Boot camp Great Lakes, ll
60	Took High School Equivalency exam and passed it
Jan–May 60	19 week US Navy Hospital Corps school Great Lakes, Ill

May	Graduated from US Navy Hospital Corps School as a proud US Navy Corpsman
60–61	US Navy Naval Hospital Newport, RI
62	US Navy X-Ray School Naval Hospital Chelsea, Mass
62–63	US Navy Naval Hospital Newport, RI
63–65	US Navy NSA Sigonella, Sicily
66	US Navy ship, USS Bushnell in Key West, FL/ Charleston, SC
66–69	US Navy, NSA Sigonella, Sicily
69–75	US Civil Service NSA Sigonella, Sicily
75	US Civil Service Warminster, PA
75–79	US Civil Service MTMC Washington (Falls Church, VA)
79	**Graduated with a BS from University of Maryland**
79–84	US Civil Service NSA Naples, Italy
84–87	US Civil Service Camp Darby Pisa, Italy
88–93	US Civil Service SETAF Vicenza, Italy
93–06	US Civil Service US Embassy Rome, Italy
06	Reluctantly retired and moved to Goshen, IN

Printed in the United States
by Baker & Taylor Publisher Services